LOUISVILLE

AND THE CIVIL WAR

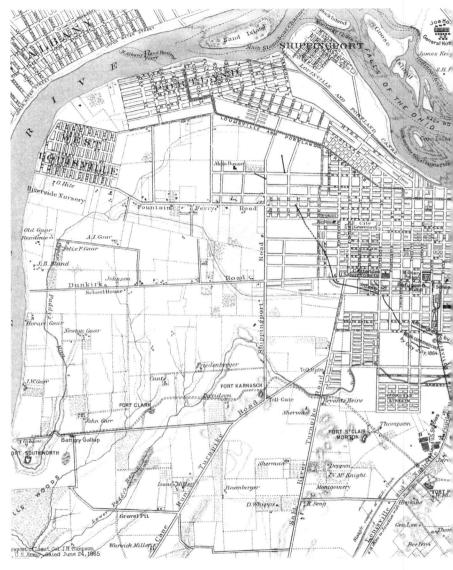

"Louisville and its Defenses." This detailed map from 1865 marks the locales of the various Union forts, camps, hospitals and prisons.

LOUISVILLE
AND THE CIVIL WAR
A HISTORY & GUIDE

BRYAN S. BUSH

Charleston   London

THE
History
PRESS

Published by The History Press
Charleston, SC 29403
www.historypress.net

First published 2008

Manufactured in the United States

ISBN 978.1.59629.554.4

Library of Congress Cataloging-in-Publication Data

Bush, Bryan S., 1966-
  Louisville and the Civil War : a history and guide / Bryan S. Bush.
    p. cm.
  Includes bibliographical references and index.
  ISBN 978-1-59629-554-4 (alk. paper)
  1. Louisville (Ky.)--History--Civil War, 1861-1865. 2. Louisville (Ky.)--Guidebooks.
  3. Historic sites--Kentucky--Louisville--Guidebooks. I. Title.
  F459.L8B87 2008
  917.69'44043--dc22
                                    2008035254

Notice: The information in this book is true and complete to the best of our knowledge. It is offered without guarantee on the part of the author or The History Press. The author and The History Press disclaim all liability in connection with the use of this book.

*Special thanks must go to: Elvin Smith Jr.;
the Louisville Free Public Library;
the University of Louisville Library;
my parents, Carol Bush and Gene Bush;
and JoAnn Bush.*

Contents

Introduction

B efore the Civil War, Louisville became a vibrant city with the help of steamboat traffic and the rise of the Louisville and Nashville Railroad. Factories emerged in the city to build rails and farm implements. Louisville manufactured hemp for cotton bags and rope. It became the second-largest city to pack pork, slaughtering 300,000 hogs a year. Louisville had industrial ties with the North and slave market ties with the South. When the Civil War erupted upon the landscape, Louisville became a military target because of the Portland Canal and the Louisville and Nashville Railroad.

Late in 1861, Confederate forces, under Kentucky native Simon Buckner, headed toward Louisville, throwing the citizens and Union military authorities into panic in the fear that the Confederates would invade the city. In August 1862, Confederate General Braxton Bragg took his army into Kentucky and poised it to take Louisville. In 1863, Confederate General John Hunt Morgan led a daring raid into Kentucky and headed for Louisville. Again, the city was on the verge of invasion. In 1864, a new threat faced the city, a threat from within the state: guerilla warfare. Almost every day, the *Louisville Journal* reported guerilla attacks. Union authorities dealt a heavy hand to control the guerilla activity, but the heavy-handed tactics only isolated the citizens of Louisville, and they began to reject both Union authority and the Lincoln administration.

This guidebook will highlight some of the important events, locations and people in Louisville during the Civil War. It will also enlighten the reader about how important the city was during the Civil War and allow the reader to trace the footsteps of the soldiers, their commanders and civil leaders.

Chapter 1

Happy Times, but Dark Clouds Gather

An Overview of Antebellum Louisville

In 1850, Louisville became the tenth-largest city in the United States. Louisville's population rose from ten thousand in 1830 to forty-three thousand in 1850. This swelling of the population can be attributed to several factors and can also help explain why the river city was such a crucial territory at the outset of the Great War.

The city became an important tobacco market and pork-packing center. Louisville's wholesale trade totaled $20 million in sales. The Louisville–New Orleans river route held top rank on the entire Western river system in freight and passenger traffic.[1] The river accounted for all of Louisville's success.

In August 1855, Louisville citizens greeted the arrival of the locomotive Hart County on Ninth and Broadway, and the first passengers arrived by train on the Louisville and Frankfort Railroad. James Guthrie, president of the Louisville and Frankfort, pushed the railroad along the Shelbyville Turnpike (Frankfort Avenue), through Gilman's Point (St. Matthews) and on to Frankfort. The track entered Louisville on Jefferson Street and ended at Brook Street.

Leven Shreve, a Louisville civic leader, became the first president of the Louisville and Nashville Railroad. With the railroad, Louisville could manufacture furniture and export the goods to Southern cities. Louisville was well on its way to becoming an industrial city. The Louisville Rolling Mill built girders, rails and

An 1855 view of East Main Street.

Louisville-made cotton machinery, all of which it sold to Southern customers. Louisville built steamboats, and the city emerged as a leader in the ironworking industry, with a plant on Tenth and Main called Ainslie, Cochran and Company.

Louisville also manufactured hemp rope and cotton bagging. Cotton bagging was made of hemp, and hemp was also used to bale cotton. Hemp was Kentucky's leading agricultural product from 1840 to 1860, and Louisville became the nation's leading hemp market. Louisville also made jean cloth for the slave market. The business area of the city stretched from Water Street (now River Road) to East (or Brook), Market and Seventh Streets. Louisville's main commerce broke down into wholesale groceries, dry goods houses and drug wholesalers. The city had eight pork houses, which slaughtered and packed 300,000 hogs a year. Tobacco outranked meatpacking as Louisville's chief product, and the three main warehouses were located at Boone, Pickett and Ninth Streets.

Dennis Long and Company was the largest pipe-manufacturing company in the West. The cement manufactured in the city was the best in the country. The Rolling Mill Company was the largest in the city. B.F. Avery & Company, Munn's and Brinly, Dodge and

Company made many of the plows in the South and Southwest. The Peter Bradas Company made cough drops from a formula supplied by Jenny Lind. Cornwall and Brother made soap and candles. The city also introduced glycerin into its commerce. Needham's Marble Shop carried Italian, Egyptian, Irish and Sienna marble. McDermott and McGrain made a cooking stove called the "Durable Kentuckian." John Bull made his Fluid of Sarsaparilla and sold his drink to New Mexico and Cuba. Hays, Craig and Company made the city's finest furs and peltries. The largest printing company in Louisville was John P. Morton and Company. Alfred Victor and Antoine Bidermann du Pont's paper mill, located at Tenth and Rowan Street, manufactured the paper used by the printing and publishing company.[2]

The steamboat route from Louisville to New Orleans held the top position for Western river freight and passenger traffic, and the Louisville–Cincinnati route was the most crowded and most prestigious. Between August 25, 1848, and August 31, 1849, sixty-six different steamboats made 213 trips from Louisville to New Orleans. Between July 1854 and October 1855, the Louisville shipbuilders constructed forty-one steamers. The steamboat industry employed 350 men, who built twenty-two boats a year and repaired another fifty. The Louisville Rolling Mill made boilers and machinery for the construction of the steamboats. A new industry began to take shape in the city. By the mid-1850s, Ainslie, Cochran and Company built a plant in order to meet the ever-demanding supply for steam engines, cotton gin machinery, wheels and castings for railroad cars and claimed its plant was the largest in the West.[3]

Railroads began to overtake steamboats. In 1850, the city chartered the Louisville and Nashville Railroad. Louisville had connections with Cincinnati, Pittsburgh, St. Louis, Memphis, Vicksburg and New Orleans. A river ferry to Jeffersonville or New Albany connected with the rail lines extending to St. Louis and Missouri, east of Pittsburgh and north to the Great Lakes. Louisville also had lines extending to Memphis, Nashville and Knoxville. The line to Lexington eventually extended to Virginia. The Louisville railroad also linked with the Baltimore and Ohio Railroad. Other rail lines that ran to Louisville were those of the Louisville, New

Former rails of the Louisville and Portland Railroad, built in 1838. The rails are located in front of the Frazier International History Museum on Main Street.

Albany and Chicago Railroad, which ran two trains daily to St. Louis, Chicago and Cincinnati.

When Louisville connected with Nashville, Louisville became the "gateway to the South." James Guthrie took control of the Louisville and Nashville Railroad in 1860 and opened the railroad to 269 miles. Guthrie planned to drain the ponds and set up a better sanitary system. As Kentucky's commonwealth attorney, he was able to push through many reforms. As a member of the state legislature, he managed to grant access for several turnpike companies and push through the construction of roads and the canal. He was the director, and later president, of the Bank of Kentucky, which was instrumental in making the Louisville Medical Institute a part of the University of Louisville. He also was a Democrat who served in the Kentucky legislature for twenty years and ran for the United States Senate several times. He was secretary of the treasury under President Pierce, and served as president of the University of Louisville in 1847.

Another view of the L&P rails.

Louisville also had three packet companies connecting it with Cincinnati, Nashville and New Orleans. Five stage routes ran to Taylorsville, Bardstown, Shelbyville and Frankfort, Shawneetown and Nashville.

The city established a board of health, enacting a College of Physicians and Surgeons, and was home to four hospitals. One of the city's hospitals was St. Joseph's Infirmary, located on the east side of Fourth, between Chestnut and Broadway. The Louisville Marine, or the City Hospital, was located on Chestnut between Preston and Floyd. Two hospitals were located in Portland—the first, the United States Marine Hospital, was located on High Street and was constructed in the 1840s; the second was the Alms House, located on Twenty-eighth and Duncan. The St. John's Eruptive Hospital was located on the Seventh Street Turnpike.

Between 1850 and 1860, the first telegraphic communication between Louisville and New Orleans was established, and the first mule-drawn streetcars were put into service. In 1854, Louisville formed the Louisville Water Company, and in 1857, work began on a reservoir and pumping station. A total of twenty-six miles of pipes were laid in the area between Main, Ninth, Broadway and Preston. On October 15, 1860, the city turned on the two steam engines manufactured by Louisville's Roach and Long Foundry, which began to pump water into the pipes.

The city boasted several cultural centers, including the Masonic Temple at Green (now Liberty) and Mozart Hall on Fourth and Jefferson. There were also horse races, fairs, musical societies and literary clubs. The Louisville Theater was located on Fourth and Green and allowed both black and white patrons. The city held agricultural fairs and exhibitions, such as the Tobacco Fair and the Southwestern Agricultural and Mechanical Association Fair. For those who loved horse races, the city offered the Woodlawn Race Course. The Du Pont Artesian Well, located on Main and Twelfth, offered hundreds of citizens the chance to partake of the healthy waters. For sports, the city offered the YMCA, the Baseball Club, a Mechanics Library and gambling.

On April 6, 1851, Jenny Lind, the Swedish Nightingale, arrived in Louisville to sing at the Mozart Theater. A coach of appointed citizens met her ten miles outside the city and hitched her four white horses to her carriage. Draped with flags, many of the buildings honored her arrival. Welcoming crowds cheered, and children with flowers greeted her as she departed her carriage for the house arranged for her two-day engagement in Louisville. She sang "The Last Rose of Summer" for the crowd.[4]

Louisville had three newspapers before the war. The *Louisville Courier* and the *Louisville Journal* were both located between Third and Fourth Streets. George Prentice founded the *Louisville Journal*. He was a member of the Whig Party and later the American Party. He loved the Union, although he supported slavery. Walter Halderman owned the *Louisville Courier* and supported the Kentucky Democrats. The official editor of the newspaper after 1859 was Colonel Robert McKee. The third newspaper was the *Louisville Democrat*, which was owned and edited by John H. Harney and supported the Northern Democrats. The paper was one of the few in the South that was antislavery.

An 1834 view of the Louisville Hotel on Main Street, looking east from Seventh Street. The hotel was rebuilt in 1853.

Fifteen hotels occupied Louisville at the time. At Second and Main was the famous Galt House. The National Hotel was located at Fourth and Main, the Louisville Hotel was located on Main and Sixth Street and the United States Hotel was located on Eighth and Main.[5]

Louisville had two hundred taverns or coffeehouses. One of the better restaurants was Pargney's at 412 Third Street. W.A. Clark served European meals at his home on Fourth, between Main and Market. The Crystal Palace at Fifth and Jefferson supplied merchants, hotels and families. The two most exclusive eateries were C.C. Ruefer's at St. Charles Restaurant at 203 Fifth Street and Walkers, or Cauweins, at 231 Third Street. Located on Seventh and Jefferson was Hafer's Ice Cream Saloon.[6]

In 1854, Louisville engineers moved the channel of the Beargrass Creek from where the creek flowed into the Ohio River between Third and Fourth Streets to the creek's present position opposite Towhead Island.

Louisville had been the first city in the West to be supplied with gas and the fifth in the country. By 1859, there were thirty-five miles of mains and 925 streetlights. The city also had seven hundred miles of streets, alleys and sidewalks.

A 1859 view of the waterfront and bridge over the Beargrass Creek at Second Street.

By 1860, Louisville's population increased to 69,739, of which 4,903 were slaves. There were 26,120 foreign-born residents, with half of them coming from Germany.[7] By 1860, the Jefferson County Courthouse was completed, and Joel T. Hart provided a statue of Henry Clay in the rotunda. In 1858, the city completed the custom house and post office at the southwest corner of Third and Liberty. The Louisville and Portland Canal underwent improvements to allow larger steamboats. The city wharf also underwent renovations.[8]

In January 1860, the city board passed a street railroad ordinance. The Louisville and Portland Company added new railcars to their lines.

By 1860, Louisville had several Catholic churches, including St. Aloysius, Notre Dame du Port, St. Boniface, St. Patrick's, St. John's and the Cathedral of the Assumption. The Episcopal Church had Christ Church Cathedral or St. Paul's. In 1860, the Calvary Church was built.

The Walnut Street Baptist Church at Fourth and Walnut had 478 members in 1860. The German Evangelical Lutherans established the St. Paul's Church on Preston and Green. The Unitarians built a church at Fifth and Walnut, and the Jewish congregation established its church on Fourth, just south of Green.

As for schools, Louisville had fifteen schools with 134 teachers. Louisville had Male High School. The General Assembly legalized the name as the Academical Department of the University of Louisville. A four-year classical course was offered to students in obtaining a BA, and an English course was recommended to those who wanted to become architects, engineers and manufacturers. A BS degree was offered on completion of the course.

The Female High School was located on Ninth and Chestnut. There were also several private schools, including the English and German Academy, B.B. Huntoon's School for Boys, Mrs. Lanham's Female Academy, the Locust Grove Academy, Mrs. Eliza Field's Female School, the Reverend George Beckett's Institution for Young Ladies, the Louisville Mercantile Academy and the Louisville Commercial College.

The University of Louisville was located on Eighth and Chestnut and comprised the School of Law and Medicine. The Law School was one of six in the country that required two years of study for the degree. The Kentucky Medical School, located on Fifth and Green, was considered one of the most elegant colleges in the country.

Louisville citizens also enjoyed Jacob's Woods, located south of Broadway between First and Fourth, and Preston's Woods at Broadway and Underhill. The Phoenix Hill Brewery was also a favorite hangout for Louisville citizens.

Louisville had eight banks, with a capital of $9,530,000. The three largest were the Bank of Louisville, the Bank of Kentucky and the Commercial Bank. Bankers' row was located on Main Street, between Second and Fifth Streets.

Emigrants from Germany and Ireland flowed into the city. By 1850, 359,980 immigrants arrived in America, and by 1854, 427,833 immigrants arrived to seek out a new living. With the arrival of massive amounts of immigrants into the city, native Louisville residents began to harbor anti-foreign, anti-Catholic sentiments. In 1841, the rise in the number of Catholics entering the city prompted the archdiocese to move the bishop's seat from Bardstown to Louisville. The archdiocese began construction on a new Catholic Cathedral in Louisville and completed the work in 1852.

In 1843, a new party arose on the political scene called the American Republican Party. On July 5, 1845, the American Republican Party changed its name to the Native American Party and held its first national convention in Philadelphia. The party opposed liberal immigration. On June 17, 1854, the Order of the Star Spangled Banner held its second national convention in New York City, featuring members composed of "native Americans" and anti-Catholics. When members answered questions about the group, they responded with "I know nothing about it," earning the moniker "Know-Nothing" Party. The new political party gained national support. The Know-Nothing Party encouraged and tapped into the nation's prejudice and fear that Catholic immigrants would take control of the United States and hand the nation over to the pope. By 1854, the Know-Nothings gained control of Jefferson County's government.

The ethnic tension came to a boil in 1855, during the election for mayor's office. On August 6, 1855, Louisville experienced "Bloody Monday," in which Protestant mobs bullied immigrants away from the polls and began rioting in Irish and German neighborhoods. Protestant mobs attacked and slaughtered at least twenty-two people. The rioting began at Shelby and Green Streets (Liberty) and progressed through the city's East End. The mob burned houses on Shelby Street and headed for William Ambruster's brewery, in the triangle between Baxter Avenue and Liberty Street, and set the place ablaze. Ten Germans were burned to death. Quinn's Irish Row, on the north side of Main between Eleventh and Twelfth Streets, was set on fire. Some of the tenants were burned to death, while others were killed by rifle fire. The Know-Nothing Party won the election in Louisville and in many other Kentucky counties.[9]

Slavery also became the topic of discussion among Louisville citizens. With the Kansas-Nebraska Act of 1854, slavery became a hot issue among politicians. The 1792 Kentucky Constitution legalized slavery, and by 1800, the tax lists showed forty thousand

A historical marker on slave trading in Louisville, located on the southeastern corner of Second and Main.

A historical marker discussing the slave pens, located on First Street between Market and Jefferson Streets.

The reverse side of the historical marker located on First Street, discussing the slavery laws in Kentucky.

slaves in Kentucky. By 1808, the federal government banned the slave trade, but the selling of women, children and men continued. By 1830, blacks made up 24 percent of Kentucky's population.

The Non-Importation Act of 1833 halted the transfer of blacks for resale, but Kentucky repealed the act in 1849, and slave markets expanded in Kentucky. The Arterburn brothers kept slave pens near Second Street, between Market and Main Streets, and iron-barred coops held slaves ready to be shipped south. Chained slaves marched up Main Street to board the boats in Portland to be shipped to New Orleans. Although slavery was on the way out in Louisville by 1850, the city sold an increasing volume of Kentucky slaves south. Kentucky annually exported between twenty-five hundred and four thousand slaves.

A posting for runaway slaves in the October 1861 *Louisville Journal.*

Amazingly, Louisville also had a free black population, and a handful managed to acquire property. Washington Spradling, freed from slavery in 1814, became a barber, and by the 1850s, he owned property valued at $30,000. In 1857, free blacks and slaves held a New Year's Eve Ball and rented the facilities from the Fall City Hotel. Louisville was a city that had characteristics of both the agricultural South and the industrial North.

Chapter 2

1860

In 1860, Kentuckians owned 225,000 slaves, with Louisville's slaves composing 7.5 percent of the population. Still, many Kentuckians also bestowed their allegiances to the Union, and it seemed that many preferred to preserve slavery *and* stay in the Union. As the 1860 presidential election drew closer, Louisville citizens were torn over the issue of slavery.

Even the newspapers began to take sides in the heated debate. Both the *Louisville Journal* and the *Louisville Courier* supported slavery, but the *Louisville Democrat* did not support the institution. Both the *Journal* and the *Democrat* supported the Union, but the *Courier* supported secession. After June 1860, the three papers supported different candidates. The *Democrat* supported James Guthrie. Unfortunately for Guthrie, the Democratic Convention held in Charleston split over the issue of slavery. The *Journal* supported John Bell of Tennessee. The *Courier* supported John C. Breckinridge, a Southern Democrat who backed secession. The Northern Democrats supported Stephen Douglas of Illinois.

In the November 1860 presidential election, Kentucky gave native Kentuckian Abraham Lincoln less than 1 percent of the vote. Kentuckians did not like Lincoln because he stood for the eradication of slavery and his Republican Party aligned itself with the North. But Kentuckians also did not vote for native son John C. Breckinridge and his Southern Democratic Party, which most of the country regarded as secessionist. Most Kentuckians, including residents of Louisville, voted for John Bell of Tennessee, of the Constitutional Unionists Party, which stood for preserving the Union and keeping the status quo on slavery; or Illinois' Stephen Douglas, who ran for the Democratic Party ticket. Louisville cast 3,823 votes for John Bell. Douglas received 2,633 votes.

On December 20, 1860, South Carolina was the first state to secede from the Union, creating a stark division of sentiment amongst Louisville's population. On February 22, 1861, the pro-Union citizens of Louisville decided to celebrate George Washington's birthday. Union flag raising spread throughout the city, and Louisville became known as "the City of Flags."[10] The event took on a whole new meaning with the political affairs. The citizens of Louisville decided to raise the national flag with pomp and circumstance over the Jefferson County Courthouse. Fifty thousand people attended the event. At 2:30 p.m., the Louisville battalions formed on Jefferson Street, fronting the courthouse. After a short prayer, James Speed delivered a patriotic speech. In his speech, he told the crowd:

The raising of the Union flag over the Jefferson County Courthouse on Washington's birthday, February 1861.

The uniform of Louisville native Union Brigadier General William Woodruff of the Union Second Kentucky Volunteer Infantry. *Courtesy of the Civil War Battles of the Western Theater Museum, Bardstown, Kentucky.*

In contemplating the causes which may disturb our Union, it occurs as a matter of serious concern, that any ground should have been furnished for characterizing parties by geographical discriminations, Northern and Southern, Atlantic and Western, whence designing men may endeavor to excite a belief that there is a real difference of local interests and views. One of the expedients of party to acquire influence, within particular district, is to misrepresent the opinions and alms of their districts. You cannot shield yourself too much against the jealousies and heart burnings which spring from their misrepresentations. They tend to alien to each other those who ought to be bound together by fraternal affection...To the efficacy and permanency of your Union, a Government for the whole is indispensable. No alliance however strict between the parts can be an adequate substitute.

And now our flag of our country what shall, what can I say equal to what we all feel. It seems surrounded with peril, and is threatened to be rent in twain. Men of America, be not discouraged! A cloud of prejudice and a storm of passion may for a time obscure its luster, but the cloud will vanish, the storm must

Brigadier General William Woodruff's elaborate engraved sword, with a portrait of Washington on the blade. *Courtesy of the Civil War Battles of the Western Theater Museum, Bardstown, Kentucky.*

abate, and as when the tempest in the material world is passed, and we look out and up, we find the heavens all star-studded, so when the political clouds and storms now about us shall pass away, we will find the flag of our country floating proudly on the breeze, bright and enduring as the heavens above.[11]

At the end of James Speed's speech, Colonel J.H. Harvey and George D. Prentice, editor of the *Louisville Journal*, raised the national flag over the courthouse. Colonel William Woodruff and the Marion Rifles, a Louisville militia company, fired three volleys from their muskets. When the citizens of Louisville raised the flag, General Simon B. Buckner, commander of the Kentucky State Guard, gave no order to salute as required by the published program and patriotic duty. Buckner and a large portion of his command moved from the Jefferson County Courthouse yard. Major William Woodruff saluted the national colors.[12] The Kentucky State Guard and the local pro-Union militias began to divide over which side the state would chose—Union or Confederate.

Chapter 3

War!

On April 12, 1861, the Civil War began when Confederate General P.G.T. Beauregard fired upon Fort Sumter in the Charleston, South Carolina harbor. Fort Sumter, commanded by Louisville native Union General Robert Anderson, surrendered to the Confederates. On April 17, 1861, Louisville hoped to remain neutral. It spent $50,000 for the defense of the city and appointed a military board to regulate and disburse the funds.

On April 20, 1861, two companies from Louisville, under the command of Captains Ben Anderson and Fred Van Alstine, left for New Orleans and were later joined by Captain Jack Thompson's company. They became the Third Kentucky Battalion. The City Guard formed in Louisville, and the Island House Guard formed in Shippingport. The Kentucky Riflemen came from the First and Second Wards of Louisville. At Male High School, a company of University of Louisville cadets took up arms.[13] On April 25, Captain Joe Desha and one hundred men from Harrison County, along with three companies from Louisville under Captains John Pope, J.B. Harvey and Michael Lapielle, left the state to join the Confederate army. They were joined in Nashville by two companies from southwest Kentucky. Others joined the Union army in Indiana or Ohio.[14] Governor Magoffin asked for $10,000 in loans from the Bank of Louisville and the Commercial Bank to ready the city of war.[15]

On May 19, Mayor Delph reported that eighteen companies of men had been voluntarily organized for the defense of the city, and he appointed Lovell Rousseau as brigadier general of the Home Guard.

The next day, on May 20, 1861, Kentucky declared its neutrality. An important state geographically, Kentucky had the Ohio River as a natural barrier. Kentucky's natural resources, manpower and the Louisville and Nashville Railroad (L&N) made both the North and South respect its neutrality. President Abraham Lincoln knew the importance of Kentucky and did not want to push the state into the other camp, so he treated Kentucky with a gentle hand. Lincoln made the statement, "I think to lose Kentucky is nearly the same as to lose the whole game. Kentucky gone, we cannot hold Missouri, nor, I think, Maryland."

Even though Kentucky's neutrality aided the Confederacy, Lincoln did little to stop the shipments of military supplies heading south by rail and river. The L&N's depot on Ninth and Broadway in Louisville, and the steamboats at Louisville's wharves, sent uniforms, lead, bacon, coffee and war material to Tennessee, Alabama, Georgia and other Southern states. Crop failures in the Southern states the previous year prompted the L&N to ship supplies to these Southern markets at an ever-increasing rate. Union troops blocked the Mobile and Ohio Railroad from sending provisions south, so the Louisville and Nashville Railroad became the only outlet for supplies in the South. Prices began to soar, and Northern businessmen made fortunes overnight. Residents of Louisville feared that all the food would be sent south, leaving them with nothing to eat, so some of the citizens tore up the Nashville tracks to prevent shipments. L&N President James Guthrie had to place armed guards on the tracks to prevent further damage.[16]

In May 1861, Lovell H. Rousseau and Lieutenant William "Bull" Nelson, a commander in the United States Navy from Maysville, worked together to strengthen the Union cause in Kentucky. Lieutenant Nelson gained an interview with Lincoln, and they discussed the situation in Kentucky. The president worried about the possibility of the well-armed State Guard, under Simon Buckner, being transferred to the Southern cause, leaving the loyal citizens of Kentucky without a means of enforcing the will of the Union-held legislature.

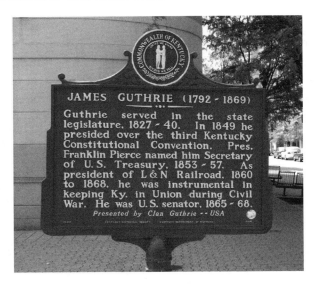

A historical marker located on Fourth and Guthrie Streets discussing James Guthrie's career.

The reverse side of the historical marker dedicated to James Guthrie.

Louisville native Union
General Lovell Rousseau.

Nelson persuaded Lincoln to send arms to Union sympathizers in Kentucky. Lincoln arranged for five thousand guns to be secretly shipped from Washington, D.C., to Louisville, with Nelson carrying out the mission. Lincoln charged Salmon Chase with the care of Nelson's work, drawing up his orders and providing the money to buy the weapons. On May 4, Nelson left with the guns by train for Louisville. At Cincinnati, he sent twelve hundred guns by steamboat to Jeffersonville, Indiana. Nelson arrived in Louisville, after leaving the remainder of the guns in Cincinnati. Lincoln directed Nelson to meet with Joshua Speed for the distribution of the weapons.[17] Joshua Speed and Lincoln had met in 1837 in Springfield, Illinois, and continued to remain close friends throughout their lives. Lincoln leaned heavily on Joshua and his brother, James Speed, to help him keep Louisville and the rest of Kentucky in Union hands.

Nelson arrived at Joshua Speed's home on Second Street, between Liberty and Walnut, but hesitated for a moment, then walked on. Several steps down the street, he turned around and headed back for Joshua Speed's house, only to pass by the house again. Inside

Louisville native James Speed, born at the Farmington Plantation, was a friend of President Abraham Lincoln and later became his attorney general in 1864.

the house, Mrs. Fanny Speed and the servants became alarmed at Nelson's pacing back and forth in front of their window. After Nelson made sure that he was not being followed, he knocked on Speed's door. One of the servants informed Nelson that Speed was in his office, several blocks away, on Jefferson Street between Fourth and Fifth Streets. When Nelson arrived at Speed's office, he shut the door and asked if they were alone. Speed assured him that no one else was in the room. Nelson asked if they might move into another room in the office. Speed agreed. Nelson introduced himself and announced his instructions from Lincoln. He explained his shipments of weapons and said that he hoped Speed would be able to distribute the guns to Unionists in the state.[18]

Speed agreed to help distribute the weapons and decided that a Unionist strategy session must take place that evening. Accompanied by his brother James, Speed left for Frankfort that afternoon by train, but he traveled separately from his brother and Nelson so

Joshua Speed, brother of James Speed, was President Abraham Lincoln's most devoted and best friend. He met Lincoln in 1837 and remained his friend until Lincoln's death in 1865.

as not to arouse suspicion. Upon arrival at the Capitol Hotel in Frankfort, Nelson visited a friend's house, while Joshua sent notice of their arrival and plans to several prominent Unionist leaders.

At 9:00 p.m. Nelson, James and Joshua met with James Harlan, John J. Crittenden, Charles Wickliffe, Garrett Davis and Thornton Marshall. The members agreed to the plan for arming Kentucky Unionists. Nelson thought that the guns should be brought into the state immediately, openly if necessary. The others disagreed, pointing out that the shipment of weapons into the state was illegal and might prove embarrassing to the Union cause. Joshua suggested that the operation remain secret until enough of the weapons had been placed in the right hands in order to secure Kentucky's future within the Union. The members agreed and decided that Joshua Speed should make the arrangements for the distribution of the weapons and that all orders for weapons given by selected men in various sections of the state must be countersigned by him. They also agreed that each member should be assigned a district, in which to distribute the weapons. In addition, they agreed to send James Speed to Indianapolis to obtain ammunition from Governor Oliver P. Morton. Morton met with James and agreed to supply ammunition to Jeffersonville, Indiana.[19]

Nelson moved the shipment of weapons from Jeffersonville to the basement of the Jefferson County Courthouse. He also sent a small shipment of weapons to Shelbyville, about forty miles southeast of Louisville, and to Hopkinsville. Nelson moved the weapons in Cincinnati to Covington. On May 17, after the weapons arrived in Covington, Nelson transported the weapons by train, bound for Cynthiana, Paris and Lexington. After the train arrived at the various depots, Unionists would distribute the weapons to other parts of the state. Garrett Davis of Kentucky sent fifteen hundred arms to Fleming and Mason Counties, two hundred to Boyd, two hundred to Greenup, one hundred to Montgomery, one hundred to Bath, one hundred to Clark, one hundred to Madison, two hundred to Fayette, two hundred to Scott, three hundred to Bourbon and five hundred to the city of Covington.

Southern sympathizers at Cynthiana learned of the shipment of "Lincoln guns" arriving at their depot and decided to capture them. As the train approached the depot, the conductor saw the huge crowd, stopped the train and returned to Covington, where the weapons were divided again. Some were sent to Maysville, and the rest remained in Covington. Unionists sent the guns in Maysville to various points in central Kentucky by wagon.[20] Kentucky historian Thomas Clark noted that Abraham Lincoln, along with Joshua and James Speed and many other shrewd Kentuckians, "succeeded in a covert way in invading the state without technically violating its neutrality. The people themselves carried out the invasion."[21]

On May 20, 1861, Governor Beriah Magoffin issued an armed neutrality proclamation and warned both Confederate and Union sympathizers to stop the acts of war on Kentucky soil. The Confederacy immediately recalled its recruiting agents from the state. Five days later, on May 25, the Louisville Home Guard formed two regiments, with Mayor Delph as commander in chief and Lovell Rousseau as brigadier general. The Federal government created the Military Department of Kentucky and placed Robert Anderson as commander. The Louisville General Council authorized Albert Fink to purchase arms for the defense of Louisville. He traveled to the Tredegar Foundry in Richmond, Virginia, to buy one 12-pound brass cannon, a 6-pounder gun, one 24-pounder and one 12-pounder siege gun and one eight-inch howitzer. The city ordered 32,027 cartridges and 4,078 pounds of lead.[22]

In June, the Home Guard camped at Camp Joe Holt in Indiana, and the University of Louisville cadets camped at Gaults Woods, two miles east of the city. The men heading for the Union enlisted at Camp Clay, across the Ohio River from Newport, or at Camp Joe Holt. Rousseau resigned from the Home Guard and formed his own brigade for the Union army.

On August 24, 1861, General Lovell Rousseau and the Louisville Legion left Camp Joe Holt, crossed the river, marched through the streets of Louisville and accepted a flag made for them by Fannie Speed, wife of Joshua Speed, and the loyal citizens of Louisville. Neutrality eroded throughout the state. The citizens of Louisville and the rest of Kentucky watched nervously to see who would make the first step to take Kentucky. The state would not have to wait long—on September 4, 1861, the Confederates invaded Kentucky.

Captain James Gorsuch of the Armstrong Rifles took the steamer *Masonic Gem* at Portland, carrying with him all their guns, ammunition and supplies, and headed for the Confederacy. On that same day, Confederate General Leonidas Polk broke Kentucky's neutrality by invading Columbus. As a result of the Confederate invasion, Union General Ulysses S. Grant entered Paducah. Confederate President Jefferson Davis allowed Confederate troops to stay in Kentucky. Confederate General Albert Sidney Johnston, commander of all Confederate forces in the West, sent Confederate General Simon Bolivar Buckner of Kentucky to invade Bowling Green. With twenty thousand troops, Confederate General Albert Sidney Johnston established a defensive line stretching from Columbus, in western Kentucky, under the command of General Leonidas Polk, to the Cumberland Gap, controlled by Confederate General Felix Zollicoffer. On September 6, 1861, Louisville native Union General Robert Anderson, moved his headquarters to Louisville.

Louisville native Union General Robert Anderson, hero of Fort Sumter, district commander in 1861.

On September 9, 1861, the Kentucky legislature asked that Anderson be made commander of the Federal military forces in Kentucky. The Union army accepted the Louisville Legion at Camp Joe Holt in Indiana into the regular army. Major John Delph sent two thousand men to build defenses around the city of Louisville. On September 15, 1862, Curran Pope became colonel of the Fifteenth Kentucky Union Infantry.

On September 17, the first trains arrived at Bowling Green, with about two thousand Confederate soldiers from Camp Boone. Buckner's Confederate troops took possession of the depot and tore down the Union flag. Buckner assembled a force of forty-five hundred men. The Confederate troops under Colonel Roger Hanson headed for the Green River and occupied Munfordville. A portion of the forces headed as far north as Elizabethtown. General William T. Sherman and Richard W. Johnson took command of the Home Guard. General Rousseau crossed the river, arriving with twenty-three companies of the Fifth Kentucky or Louisville Legion to assist General Sherman.

The arrival of the Forty-ninth Ohio Infantry as they march past the Louisville Hotel, October 19, 1861.

On September 23, 1861, the Forty-ninth Ohio, under the command of Colonel Gibson, arrived in Louisville to embark on the Louisville and Nashville Railroad. They paraded through the streets, and the Union men and women came out to greet the soldiers. The regiment stopped to pay their respects to General Anderson at the Louisville Hotel. General Anderson appeared on the balcony, thanked the Ohio regiment for complimenting him and welcomed them to Louisville. He told them that they had come at a time when Kentucky needed their services and that every Kentuckian would appreciate their motives. Colonel Gibson alluded to the gallant manner in which Kentucky had come to the rescue of the frontiers of Ohio in former days and said that Ohio designed to show that it had not forgotten those services. They were here, in blood, to protect the constitutional rights of their neighbors.

The regiment left for the Nashville depot, heading for General Sherman's headquarters.[23] With the Forty-ninth Ohio came a considerable amount of soldiers who were ill, but no hospital arrangements had been made for them in the city. The sick from Rousseau's brigade from Camp Joe Holt were sent to the Marine

Hospital, but there was no space for the new soldiers. Louisville was in the process of erecting two new hospitals, but they were not ready for soldiers. The sick were taken to a lady who kept a large boardinghouse near the depot.[24]

On that same day, weapons arrived in the city—four thousand Prussian muskets—and Assistant Secretary of War T.A. Scott informed Indiana Governor Oliver Morton that another eighteen thousand guns had left the New York arsenal and were headed for Louisville.[25]

On September 27, Indiana Governor Oliver Morton wrote to General John Fremont at St. Louis requesting troops and supplies for three thousand men. He feared that Louisville could not be saved and that the city was in great danger. Morton sent four regiments to the city.[26]

By early October, Louisville had become a staging ground for Union troops heading south. Union troops flowed into Louisville from Ohio, Indiana, Pennsylvania and Wisconsin. White tents and training grounds sprang up at the Oakland track, on Eighteenth and Broadway, along the Frankfort and Bardstown Turnpikes and around the L&N tracks just south of the city, as well as in Portland.[27]

On October 6, 1861, Joshua Speed and Colonel Jeremiah Boyle returned from Washington, D.C., where they secured seventeen thousand weapons, including three thousand Enfield rifles from England, three thousand cavalry weapons and equipment, six batteries of artillery, one thousand wagons and a large amount of powder. Joshua Speed reported to the citizens of Louisville that Lincoln took a special interest in Kentucky's affairs and would do anything to aid Kentucky.

On October 8, Anderson stepped down as commander of the Department of the Cumberland, and Union General William Tecumseh Sherman took charge of the Louisville Home Guard.

By October 20, Sherman had seventeen regiments from Indiana, thirteen from Ohio, three from Pennsylvania and several other regiments in the state ready to move at a moment's notice toward the Green River or the Cumberland Gap. Two days later, on October 22, thirty-eight hundred Pennsylvania troops disembarked from six steamers and paraded through the city. Two brass bands and drum corps played martial music as they went by the hotel,

Union General William T. Sherman took over as military commander for the district of Kentucky in November 1861.

and the troops that followed passed in review by Sherman and the Galt House. Eight six-pound cannons with caissons rolled down the streets, followed by 120 horses. The troops camped near the old Oakland racetrack located on Seventh and Hill Streets.[28] The Thirty-seventh Indiana's Colonel Hazard and the Second Minnesota's Colonel Van Cleve arrived by rail, and Sherman sent them to Elizabethtown and Lebanon Junction.

By October 22, several newspapers picked up on Cameron's memorandum, stating that Sherman's request for 200,000 men was insane. The papers began to label Sherman as insane, crazy and mad.

With so many troops arriving, the city took on a military stance. At the Masonic Temple, officers taught tactics in small and broad swords and bayonets. The Union army established two new hospitals, one was located on Ninth and Broadway in a building once owned by General Simon Buckner, and the other was located

Union General Don Carlos Buell. *Courtesy of the National Archives.*

on Eighth and Broadway. Volunteer families' relief organizations, citizens' committees and the Ladies Soldiers Relief Committee all helped to give meals to soldiers and provide them with comfort and clothing.[29]

On November 6, 1861, General Sherman stepped down as commander of the Department of the Ohio, and on November 13, Union General Don Carlos Buell arrived in Louisville to replace him.

Union regiments continued to flow into the city. On November 9, Colonel Curran Pope and the Fifteenth Kentucky Union Infantry marched through the streets of Louisville. Several days later, on November 11, the First and Second Wisconsin arrived in town. On November 24, five steamers brought five thousand soldiers from Ohio. One of the regiments that arrived on the steamers was the Twenty-first Ohio Infantry.

On November 26, 1861, Alfred Searles, of the Twenty-first Ohio, wrote to E.G. Searles from his camp in Louisville that the regiment chased the Rebels almost four hundred miles and had three battles with them. He wrote that the regiment was forced to march for weeks, about fifteen to thirty miles, day and night. The regiment lived on three days' rations for eight days. He ate six crackers and one and a half pounds of meat. The crackers were "enough to sicken a hog." The soldiers went two days on nothing but a little piece of fresh pork, with no salt, roasted on a stick over the campfire. Mud was shin deep. They arrived in Louisville by riverboats and were "stowed in worse than they stow hogs in their to ship. And we were packed in that way four days." He reported that the regiment camped four miles outside of Louisville, and sixty thousand troops camped in sight of their camp. He thought the army planned to move on Memphis, Tennessee. While in camp, the regiment "have never done nothing but drill and we want rest…Our men are completely worn out. We have not got our pay that the three months pay is up today."[30]

On November 28, three more Ohio regiments landed at the wharf and camped on the Seventh Street Turnpike.[31] On December 8, 1861, Alfred Searles wrote to E.G. Searles from Camp Buell that the men in the Twenty-first Ohio Infantry had not been paid and the soldiers were "wrongly used, for the law is that they shall not be in debt to a soldier over sixty days and we are going into our fourth month." He received a second suit of clothes, which included a roundabout dress coat, a pair of pants, one cap, one pair of socks, one shirt and one pair of shoes. The regiment expected to march out, and he carried a backpack weighing sixty-five pounds.

Searles wrote that Louisville was the center of the state for the stock and provisions for the war. He reported that twelve hundred head of horses and mules were in the yards. He also wrote that a large army was in Elizabethtown. "There is over 100 there and of our men there now. And they average two regiments a day that goes through here on cars, besides what goes at other points to that place." He also wrote that the Rebels were on the Green River near Bowling Green. "There is about 25 or 30 thousand of them. They have not got much to eat and poorly clad. And they are sick too,

Union troops arriving on the Louisville wharf, 1861.

according to what they say." Searles hoped that both armies would sign a treaty, "for the fighting will be desperate after this."

By December 15, the Twenty-first Ohio marched to Camp Harris in Elizabethtown. Searles wrote that the regiment camped eight miles from the Rebel lines. The Union troops crossed the Green River, and he hoped that in a couple of days the Union army would "see old Buckner." General James Mitchell visited their camp. Searles wrote that there were seven divisions, six thousand Ohio infantry and twenty-four brass cannons, which totaled 150,000 Union soldiers.

On December 5, 1861, Guy Morgan, of the Twenty-first Ohio Volunteer Infantry, wrote to his friend Henry Hill from Camp Buell. His regiment arrived in Louisville on November 25, 1861, and he reported that the Twenty-first, Second, Thirty-third and Fifty-ninth Ohio regiments arrived in camp the same day. The Forty-first, Fifty-first, Third, Twenty-fourth and Sixth Ohio, along with the Fifteenth through Seventeenth Indiana Regiments, arrived later that day. Morgan reported that a good deal of sickness took place in the camp. The Louisville and Nashville Railroad ran past their camp. The regiment drilled for four hours a day and "have beef, crackers, coffee and sugar to live on part of the time and part of the time we have pork in place of beef."[32] On December 22 and 23, the Union army received 145 tons of ammunition in Louisville for the newly arrived troops.

Chapter 4

A Soldiers' Gathering

By January 1, 1862, Louisville had eighty thousand Union troops throughout the city. With so many troops, entrepreneurs set up gambling establishments along the north side of Jefferson from Fourth to Fifth Streets, turned the corner on Fifth Street to Market and continued on the south side of Market Street back to Fourth Street. Photography studios and military goods shops, such as Fletcher & Bennett, on Main Street, and Hirschbuhl & Sons, located on Main Street east of Third Street, catered to the Union officers and soldiers. With so many Union troops, brothels also sprung up around the city. Many of the soldiers came from small communities and had never been exposed to childhood diseases. With thousands of soldiers gathered in one area, diseases broke out among the troops. Smallpox, measles, diphtheria, rubella and whooping cough took a heavy toll on the troops. Army hospitals sprung up at Ninth and Broadway, Eighth and Green, on Main between Seventh and Eighth, at Seventh and Main, Seventh and Green and Fifteenth and Main to handle the sick.[33]

W.L. Curry, a member of the First Ohio Cavalry, wrote about his experience in Louisville. He reported that the regiment went into camp at Camp Buell, located at the Oakland racetrack, just outside the city limits. He described the camp as beautiful, "with good drill grounds, and we resumed drills and regular camp duties at once, with mounted 'dress parades' and practice marches on the pikes leading out from the city." Soon after Curry's arrival at Camp Buell, measles broke out among the men,

Union General Don Carlos Buell's bodyguard parading east on Main Street at Fifth Street in January 1862.

and as it was quite severe winter weather, many of those taken down with the disease caught cold and died, and with many others disease of throat and lungs resulted, which followed them though their army service, and in some cases through life.[34]

On January 3, 1861, Guy Morgan, of the Twenty-first Ohio Infantry, wrote to a friend from Camp Jefferson that seven men of Company K had come down with measles and spent their time in a Louisville hospital. Among them was Leonard Fair. Morgan also wrote that George Macfall, a member of the Twenty-first Ohio, had diarrhea and became so

run down with diarrhea till he was so weak that he could hardly go any more. When he was taken with the measles they give him a discharge to go home but the poor boy was too near gone then to get well. The boy inquired the night before he died of one of the boys if there wasn't some way to get him down on the boat so he could go home but he was near gone by then.[35]

On December 21, 1861, George Macfall died from disease. Morgan wrote: "This is a poor [place] for a man to be when he is sick. There is nothing here fit for a sick [man to] eat."

With eighty thousand men, the Louisville economy thrived. Soldiers bought food at the restaurants, stayed in the hotels and visited the theaters, coffee shops and saloons. But many of the troops were young men who, for the first time, were not under parental supervision, and some of the soldiers drank too much. Fights broke out in the theaters, saloons and the streets. The provost marshal forbade the sale of liquor to soldiers within five miles of camp. All coffeehouses and saloons were closed.[36]

Colonel Charles McCormick, of the Seventh Pennsylvania Cavalry, wrote to his father about the victory at Mill Springs and about camp conditions at Camp Crittenden in Jeffersonville, Indiana. On January 22, 1862, he described the muddy camp, which he claimed was

> *a perfect bed of mortar, quite thick, and well mixed by the horses feet, and without exaggerating about eight, and in some places, ten inches deep. I have seen men stick fast and lose their boots, and horses while on a walk, stumbling and fall.*

He continued, writing that the people of

> *Louisville, Jeffersonville, and the surrounding County are rejoicing over the defeat of Gen. Zollicoffer and all parties [soldiers] are anxious to move on towards Green River, and particularly anxious to get to <u>Bowling Green</u>. To you [it] might seem queer that we are all wishing to get to the place where there [is] some prospect of a little fighting, but this seems to be the case <u>invariably</u>, and it is <u>well</u> it is so.*[37]

Several days later, on January 26, 1862, McCormick's regiment crossed the river at Jeffersonville, but the crossing took several hours because of high water on the Ohio River. McCormick reported that the Ohio River was at its highest since 1844. The water backed up until the regiment was almost surrounded by water in its old camp. After they crossed the river, the soldiers marched through the city. They arrived in the city on a Sunday, and church services had been dismissed. McCormick wrote:

> *It seemed as though the whole city were out to see us. The Stars and Stripes were flying everywhere. We were <u>cheered all along the different streets</u>. Men rolled up in the American flag and where the ladies could not get flags, the white handkerchiefs had to suffice. I was told that as we passed a Catholic church, the priest sent his <u>congregation out to cheer us on</u>, and surely they did. It seemed like anything else than Sunday. I was particularly amused at Prentise of the* Louisville *Journal. He stood on the Corner of 5th and Main streets with his hat in hand, swinging his head, and as much excited as man could be. As I passed at the head of my squadron, he said, "Good bye Captain, God be with you. I will visit you on the Green River. You are the finest Regiment that has passed here," and more that I could not hear. We were highly complimented on all sides throughout the whole march.*

The 1,160 cavalrymen rode ten miles on the Bardstown Pike, along "which are very handsome country residences. Every place seemed to be supplied with stars and stripes."

McCormick also commented on the Kentucky weather. When the Seventh Pennsylvania Regiment arrived at camp, most of the soldiers did not erect tents since the weather seemed like a June day, although they were in the middle of January. By morning, the weather had changed, and three inches of snow fell on the ground. By 10:00 p.m. that night, lightning and thunder illuminated and shook the hill on which the regiment was camped.

On January 30, 1862, Guy Morgan wrote from Camp Jefferson that many of his fellow soldiers continued to fall from sickness. Although he had been inoculated for smallpox, two cases entered their regiment. Military surgeons placed the soldiers with smallpox in the woods outside the camp in their own tents. Two soldiers were later transported to a hospital in Louisville. Soldiers in his regiment came down with measles, typhoid fever and rheumatism.[38]

Union General Don Carlos Buell's headquarters, located on the west side of Fourth Street near Walnut. The Catholic Cathedral of the Assumption is in the background. Don Carlos Buell became district commander after Sherman stepped down and later became commander of the Army of the Ohio.

By February 24, Union General Don Carlos Buell had taken Bowling Green, and on March 5, 1862, he arrived in Nashville. On that same day, General Buckner and 135 prisoners arrived in Jeffersonville and were taken to an Indianapolis prison. From there they were transferred to Fort Warren prison in Boston, Massachusetts. The wounded from Fort Henry and Donelson also arrived in Louisville by steamboat. Union authorities converted the former plow manufacturing company of B.F. Avery, located on Fifteenth and Main, into a large military hospital.[39]

Although Buell took many of the regiments with him to Nashville, more regiments flowed into Louisville. By March 1, 1862, twenty-eight regiments camped around the city. Union camps sprung up at the Institution for the Blind, around Preston's Woods, along the Bardstown Road between Cave Hill Cemetery and Grinstead Drive, at the fairgrounds and in Portland, in areas south of the city.

On November 8, 1862, John Wilkes Booth played to sold-out crowds for twelve nights at the Louisville theaters. He later assassinated President Lincoln in April 1865.

The House of Refuge, now the University of Louisville campus, became the Park Barracks and contained 1,000 men.[40] With so many troops in the city, the sick accumulated in the hospitals. Trains brought the sick soldiers to the city every evening. School buildings, churches and even a few factories served as makeshift hospitals. Between January 1862 and March 1862, a total of 265 soldiers died from disease in Louisville hospitals, and 1,000 soldiers died in the first nine months of the war, but conditions improved in the city. The Union army reduced twenty hospitals down to three that could handle 2,000 patients. The Medical Department increased, and many of the volunteer services provided by the local ladies decreased.[41]

After the Battle of Shiloh, fought in April 1862, Union General Ulysses S. Grant informed Mayor Delph of Louisville to prepare for two thousand wounded soldiers. Many wounded Confederate prisoners also arrived in the city.

A view of the entrance to Cave Hill Cemetery.

Although the threat of invasion by Confederates subsided, Louisville remained a staging area for Union supplies and troops heading south. By May 1862, the steamboats arrived and departed at the wharf in Louisville with their cargoes. Military contractors in Louisville provided the Union army with two hundred head of cattle each day, and the pork packers provided thousands of hogs daily. Trains departed for the South along the L&N.

On June 1, 1862, the Union command appointed Union General Jeremiah T. Boyle as U.S. commandant of Kentucky, with his headquarters in Louisville.

In June 1862, John Wilkes Booth, who later assassinated President Abraham Lincoln in April 1865, made a return appearance in Louisville. He had visited the city in December 1861 to play for a two-week engagement. The city of Louisville loved the young, handsome actor, and he returned for another two-week performance.

By June 6, 1862, 930 soldiers had died in the military hospitals at Louisville since September 1861. The city donated a plot in Cave Hill Cemetery for any soldier who should die in Kentucky in defense of the Union. Union Captain Henry Clay, grandson of Senator Henry Clay, was buried in Cave Hill Cemetery on June 7, 1862, and his brother, Confederate Major Thomas Clay, was buried next to him a year later.[42]

Chapter 5

1862 Confederate Invasion of Kentucky

On July 31, 1862, Confederate General Braxton Bragg and Major General Edmund Kirby Smith met in Chattanooga, Tennessee, to plan their invasion of Kentucky. Both generals were hoping to bring Kentucky into the fold of the Confederacy, but neither general decided to take Lexington, Louisville, other locations on the Ohio River or the railroads. One of the objectives of the Confederate campaign in Kentucky was to seize the Louisville and Portland Canal, severing Union supply routes on the Ohio River. General P.G.T. Beauregard suggested destroying the Louisville canal so completely that "future travelers would hardly know where it was."

Braxton Bragg had high hopes for Kentucky. Kentucky Confederate Calvary General John Hunt Morgan promised that Bragg would be able to pick up 100,000 men if he entered Kentucky. Bragg needed the massive influx of troops if he was going to take the state. Bragg was also looking for badly needed supplies. General Bragg controlled the Army of Mississippi, and General Smith controlled the Army of East Tennessee. Neither general answered to the other, and they only verbally agreed to cooperate in the upcoming campaign.

The plan to invade Kentucky was doomed from the beginning because neither general had a unified movement or a clearly defined objective. Edmund Kirby Smith was the first to enter the state on August 18, 1862, and he wrote to Bragg that the country was "almost completely drained of all kinds of supplies." He wrote to his wife: "The country is desperately union and bushwackers [*sic*] have commenced operations against our detachments." He found the citizens of Kentucky "bitterly and violently opposed to us."[43] By August 29, the advance regiments began their movement north into the Bluegrass.

When the state legislature learned that the Confederate forces were headed for Frankfort, they gathered what records they could carry and the $1 million in the state treasury and left Frankfort for Louisville.[44] The General Assembly held its sessions in the Jefferson County Courthouse. Ironically, James Guthrie had built the Jefferson County Courthouse in 1830, hoping that the state capital would move to Louisville. The courthouse was not completed until 1859. The governor had his office at 521 Sixth Street, while the secretary of state and the adjutant moved in with Speed and Barret, just across Jefferson Street from the courthouse. The auditor and the treasurer were on Main Street, one door west of the Bank of Kentucky, and the quartermaster general was across the street.[45]

Kentucky Governor James Robinson told the citizens of Kentucky: "Our state has been invaded by an insolent foe…Now is the time for Kentuckians to defend themselves." General Dumont took charge of the Home Guard and immediately began to recruit new troops. James Guthrie held a meeting of the Union men and formed them into volunteer companies for home defense. An order was posted that all businesses must close at 4:00 p.m. so that the employees could drill. Federal authorities issued an announcement for all citizens who possessed government-issued muskets to turn them in immediately for arming the new soldiers.[46] The town filled with refugees, who had come to Louisville for safety, and the hotels overflowed with Union officers. The refugees came from the surrounding countryside and were driven in by the Confederate advance. An extreme drought filled the streets with dust.

On September 2, Federal authorities placed Louisville under martial law, and General Boyle ordered all males between the ages of eighteen and forty-five to enroll for drill or remain in their residences. All businesses closed at 4:00 p.m. and all saloons were shut down. The assembly of people in hotels was prohibited.[47] Louisville had few Union troops to stop the advance of Bragg and Smith. Buell's army was in Tennessee, and Bragg's army was between Buell and Louisville. The next day, on September 3, Confederate General Edmund Kirby Smith took Frankfort. His cavalrymen headed for Georgetown and Versailles. Union General Jeremiah Boyle appealed to Illinois and Indiana for troops. Panic set in among the Union generals at the Galt House at Second and Main Street.[48]

Fearing that Buell would not arrive in Louisville to prevent Bragg's army from capturing the city, Union General William Nelson ordered the construction of a hasty defensive line around the city and the placement of pontoon bridges across the Ohio to facilitate the evacuation of the city or to receive reinforcements from Indiana. Local citizens and regular Union troops built a chain of seven forts, stretching from the fairgrounds in the west to Beargrass Creek in the east. Fresh Union troops arrived in the city. Exhausted men worked by candlelight to strengthen the entrenchments. Louisville citizens feared that Bragg was free to join Smith, who occupied most of central Kentucky, and the two would throw their combined forces of fifty thousand at Louisville. Only thirty thousand Union soldiers occupied the city.

Army supplies were stacked in the warehouses at First Street and the river, wagons and harness shops spread throughout the city and the barracks at Third and Kentucky Streets were filled to capacity. Across the southern edge of the city, Union officials erected stables, corrals and forage sheds. Tent encampments surrounded the city. Military officials constructed six general hospitals, located at Ninth and Broadway, Eighth and Liberty, Sixth between Walnut and Chestnut, Seventh and Main, Fifteenth and Main and Center and Liberty. Smallpox victims were taken to a hospital on Bardstown Road, near Cave Hill Cemetery. At Union headquarters in Louisville, the generals could not decide whether to fight for the city or abandon it. More stores emptied their shelves, and the banks were beginning to empty their vaults. Household goods were piled on the wharf. Panic paralyzed the city. Owners of boats and skiffs charged high fees to ferry both people and goods to Indiana.[49]

On September 19, Nelson assumed command of the Union forces in Louisville. The next day, on September 20, General

Nelson issued the following order: "The women and children of this city will prepare to leave the city without delay." He ordered the Jeffersonville ferry to be used for military purposes only. Private vehicles were not allowed onboard the ferryboats without a special permit. Hundreds of Louisville residents gathered at the wharf to be transported to New Albany or Jeffersonville. Nelson announced that he would defend the city, but if his defenses should fail and the Rebels took Louisville, he would turn his cannons on the city and reduce it to rubble. Nelson ordered all residents who did not choose to fight to stay in their homes or risk being shot. The military impressed an army of one thousand slaves to help build the earthworks around the city.[50]

On September 21, the city ordered all the public schools closed. A fire broke out at 2:00 a.m. at the Thomas Nash tobacco factory on Broadway between Eighteenth and Main Streets. The main building burned to the ground. Four soldiers opened fire at Sixth and Main, and they claimed they were shooting at a drayman who ignored an order to halt. Rebel cavalry, hoping to destroy the bridge over the Salt River, attacked the Union outpost commanded by General R.S. Granger at Shepherdsville. General Granger beat back the Rebel cavalry, killing eight and capturing twenty-one.[51]

On September 22, 1862, a huge crowd gathered at the Jefferson County Courthouse in an eleventh-hour meeting of loyal men. Mayor John Delph appealed to Louisville men to stand and fight the approaching Rebel armies. Mayor Delph said that Louisvillians who were willing to take place in the battle line would be issued arms. He told the crowd: "If we can hold the enemy, Buell will advance on his rear and annihilate him."

At the Galt House, General Nelson threw himself into his duties. All picks and spades in the city would be seized for use in the trenches. Work on the pontoon bridges had already begun. Coal barges were lashed together, and then double tracks of planks were laid across the barges. One bridge was west of Towhead Island; the other was located at Lower Portland Landing. Two large boats were waiting at the foot of Fourth Street under orders to take aboard woman and children. The panic on the wharf reached a crescendo. Children and weeping women held one another tight. Men with

Citizens of Louisville on the wharf, fleeing the city in September 1862. Second Street is located on the left.

no taste for a siege paced among the disordered piles of household goods, baggage and military supplies. They haggled with boat owners for passage to Indiana. Refugees from Marion County met at the United States Hotel and organized a volunteer brigade. A message from the telegraph operator at La Grange warned that the Rebels had captured the Union outposts in the city. The attack on Louisville could come at any moment.

On September 24, advance units under General Don Carlos Buell's army arrived in the city. Amazingly, Bragg decided to wheel his army to the right and headed for Bardstown, Kentucky. The path to Louisville remained open to Buell's troops. On September 26, 1862, Buell's entire army arrived in Louisville, tired and hungry. The poorly equipped and exhausted Home Guard watched in awe and relief as Buell's army marched into town. Supply wagons followed behind Buell's infantry, followed by his cannons. Kentucky Union General Thomas Crittenden crossed the Salt River with twelve thousand Union troops and six batteries. Major General Alexander McCook's division marched from Bowling Green. Buell's soldiers were showered with food, water and gifts. The citizens shouted to the soldiers: "God bless you."[52]

Twelve thousand Union troops arriving from the advance army of the Army of the Ohio, September 24, 1862, along the Salt River Road (present-day Dixie Highway) as seen on Broadway, east of Eighteenth Street.

Union General Samuel Curtis's division marching past the Louisville Hotel, 1862.

Luckily, many soldiers left diaries and letters recording their experiences upon arrival in Louisville. On September 26, Captain John Tuttle and Lieutenant James Hardin, of the Third Kentucky Infantry, Company G, arrived in Louisville. In his diary, Tuttle stated that, after the men arrived in Louisville, they stacked arms and tore down a number of outhouses, fences and other structures for fuel. Captain Taylor, also of the Third Kentucky, and Captain Tuttle walked to Main Street to find something to eat. They found some cheese, crackers, sardines, sausages and whiskey. After breakfast, Lieutenant Hardin and Tuttle visited the city and purchased suits of clothes and numerous other articles "necessary for our comfort in our present condition." While in the city, the men took baths, received shaves, put on their new clothes and looked "extremely well." Hardin and Tuttle were mortified when they passed along the streets with veteran soldiers crying out, "New troops, band box soldiers, never seen hardship!" They wished they had "southern soil an inch thick all over us."[53]

The next day, on September 27, the Third Kentucky moved to the suburbs on First Street. On September 28, Tuttle and Hardin again visited the city, where they "splurged expensively" all day and returned to camp. The next day, the men went to the theater. On September 30, Captain Tuttle and Lieutenant Hardin visited the city to see the play *Lady of Lyons*.[54]

On September 7, 1862, First Lieutenant William Wirt Calkins of the 104th Illinois, arrived with his regiment at Camp Joe Holt in Jeffersonville, Indiana. There were no tents or quarters for the men. Most of the soldiers slept on the ground. The next day, the 104th Illinois bathed in the Ohio River. After breakfast, the men gained passes and visited the neighborhood farmers, who had good orchards, but Calkins pointed out that "it may be sarcasm to say they were welcomed." Calkin noted that that he stood

> on the border land between freedom and slavery, and could see just across the river "Old Kentucky" the miserable neutrality state, which had been trying so hard to get out of the Union, or else to be allowed to remain neutral, but, as Senator Stephen A. Douglas said in his last great speech at the beginning of the war, "Henceforth there can be but two parties in this country, one of the Union and the other against it," so this state had been compelled to fall into line on the right side by the prompt action of her citizens, who, in large majority, remained loyal and true, assisted by Federal bayonets.[55]

Calkins heard the rumors of General Bragg advancing into Kentucky and of General Kirby Smith's army approaching Covington. Rumors also entered camp that General Buell's army had reached Nashville and was "running a race with Bragg for Louisville." He noted the new regiments pouring into the city for days, and with the citizens pressed into service, they built earthworks and forts. The 104th Illinois remained in camp until September 14. During this time, the men received arms, uniforms, equipment and tents—Sibley tents, which held fifteen to eighteen men. The quartermaster issued the troops dark blue jackets, sky blue pants, blue overcoats with capes, woolen shirts and socks, cotton drawers

Lieutenant James Hardin's uniform and kepi. Hardin was a member of the Fifteenth Kentucky Union Infantry, but was later promoted to lieutenant in the Third Kentucky Union Infantry. He visited the city several times during the Civil War. *Courtesy of the Civil War Battles of the Western Theater Museum, Bardstown, Kentucky.*

and blue caps. Some of the uniforms were made of shoddy material, and the men cussed at the people responsible for making them.

The men heard about Munfordville and Bragg's attack on Colonel John T. Wilder's men. The regiment moved out on September 14 to an old brickyard, along with the 81st, 82nd and 87th Indiana. General Stephen Gano Burbridge commanded the whole force. The men pitched tents and cleared away the bricks. The Burbridge brigade remained at Camp Gilbert—or as the men called it, "Camp Brickbat"—until September 17, when the Union command ordered the 104th Illinois to march over the Ohio. Two ferryboats took the men to Louisville. As the men marched through Louisville, there

61

was no welcoming cheers from an eager and loyal people grateful to their deliverers from calamity; no National flags floating from the housetops. Few white people appeared, while the black population lined the sidewalks and peered from the windows. The city was under the iron grasp of martial law, and sentries walked their beats on every street. Louisville had become a vast armed camp. Thousands of soldiers and impressed citizens were still at work day and night on the defenses. The Provost Marshal compelled all white male citizens between the ages of eighteen and forty-five to drill every day or go to jail, a regulation that caused a good deal of squirming among the disloyal element.

After passing through Louisville, the 104th Illinois marched into the country for three miles and camped on the plantation of Confederate General Simon Bolivar Buckner.

The ample grounds in front of his large, fine brick residence made an admirable bivouac for the Regiments, whose ideas about such things were yet aesthetic. No place could have been more lovely; the beautiful green lawn sloped gently down from the house, and was covered with a scattered growth of noble oak and beech trees…A stonewall laid in mortar, with an iron gate, enclosed the ample grounds.

Culkins found the situation odd that, while General Buckner was in Fort Warren as a prisoner of war, the 104th Illinois guarded his property.[56] They named their new camp "Camp Robinson" or "Camp Grasshopper" because of the many grasshoppers on Buckner's lawn. On September 17, the men heard of Colonel John Wilder's surrender and feared that Bragg would "be thundering next at the gates of Louisville." Rebel prisoners brought in from the front increased the rumors and excitement in camp.[57]

Union General Henry Halleck ordered two divisions from General Ulysses S. Grant to Louisville to support Buell. Soon, the city was filled with 100,000 men. The stores in Louisville were allowed to reopen for business. Bragg urged General Smith to join his forces to take Louisville, but Smith told him to take Louisville on his own.

On September 21, General Stephen Gano Burbridge inspected the camp. Four thousand men drew "up in battle array, performing military evolutions, their burnished arms flashing in the sunlight, was well calculated to awaken pride and enthusiasm."[58] On September 22, more Rebel prisoners arrived in camp. Union soldiers captured them only ten or fifteen miles from the city. Some of the wagon drivers, or "mule whackers," reported the approach of Bragg's advance. All the country people, black and white, were fleeing in haste toward Louisville.

That night, the 104th Illinois received orders from Colonel Orlando Moore to march back into Louisville. As the soldiers marched up the road toward Louisville, several other regiments were also taking the same road, and soon it became clogged with troops. At 2:00 a.m. the regiment arrived in the city's defenses and the men slept on the breastworks. The next day, the men camped at Camp Wilder, situated on a high bluff on the eastern outskirts of the city, in a location surrounded by packinghouses and "tumbledown tenements," which emitted "offensive and disease-breeding odors."[59] Lieutenant Calkins learned that Bragg had turned his army around and was headed for Lexington. He also heard about General Buell's fifty thousand men arriving in and around Louisville.

On September 26, the regiment performed heavy detail on the fortifications, which extended along the hill southeast of the camp and ran through Cave Hill Cemetery. Calkins noted that, when the men built fortifications through the cemetery, he felt "sacrilege to thus invade the city of the dead, but military necessity often compels many things to be done that seem cruel or necessary."[60]

On September 14, 1862, John Boon, of the Eighty-fifth Illinois Infantry, arrived in Louisville and camped one mile from the city. He noticed that Louisville was a "very large place. It is five miles long on the river's edge and about two miles from the river to the south side of town. There are some very nice homes here." He also commented on the guards in the streets, who would arrest a person if he did not have a pass. He mentioned in his letter to home that there were twenty-five thousand soldiers in his camp. His regiment camped close to Cave Hill Cemetery. He told his friends that the citizens of Louisville were half Union and half Confederate. His meals consisted of meat, crackers and coffee, but "most of the boys buy cakes, pies, etc. of the women and the sutler. For my part I can't eat their grub and I live on what we have."

On September 16, the Eighty-fifth Illinois marched through Louisville. During the march, the men began to feel the effects of the heat and drought. Many came down with sunstroke. Some of the men "fell dead in the ranks, such is war." Boon's regiment marched two miles southeast of the city. He mentioned that "Louisville is the finest city I have ever seen in our trip and I would like to live here if I were able." When Boon obtained a pass, he visited Cave Hill Cemetery. He saw some nice monuments

said to cost several thousand dollars. Also some tombs where we could see the coffins through the bars at the door. I saw the tomb and coffin of the Kentucky giant [Jim Porter] said to be seven feet eight inches tall. It was covered with a stone case. Where we are now camped I can see from here a Catholic graveyard. Every grave has a cross on the headstone. It is small in comparison to Cave Hill Cemetery, which has more than eighty acres of land in it. There also is a cave adjoining but it is not much. I was in it. There were several Union soldiers buried in Cave Hill Cemetery on Sunday. There is an acre of ground with graves of Union soldiers as thick as they can be. Also fifty Secesh graves. They are better fixed than the graves of our poor boys. There have nice board head markers with names, where from, and with all on it. Our boys have a small board perfectly plain. I hope I will never be placed there.[61]

By September 21, General Buell formed the 36th Brigade and assigned the 85th Illinois Infantry, along with the 86th Illinois, 125th Illinois, 52nd Ohio Infantry and Battery I, 2nd Illinois Light Artillery, to the brigade. Colonel Daniel McCook commanded the brigade. Major General Phil Sheridan commanded the division, and Major General Charles Gilbert commanded the 3rd Corps. The 36th Brigade moved its camp three miles east of Louisville. The brigade camped in a grove of beech trees, with a creek running

A monument to Union General Lovell Rousseau, Cave Hill Cemetery.

through the camp. Boon marched a mile to a spring to get water since six thousand men were using the same water source. Rumors circulated in camp that General Bragg planned to attack the city, but Boon assured his wife that the Union army would "whip him for sure." He stated that seventy-five thousand men camped in and around the city and threw up entrenchments all around it.

The next day, Boon wrote to his comrades at home that General Bragg was marching toward the city to attack. He described the entrenchments, which were about seven miles long, but only four feet wide and three feet deep, with a step for the men to stand on to shoot the advancing Confederates. He again told his friends there were seventy-five thousand men, with twenty-five thousand enrolled under martial law. He noticed five gunboats patrolling the river. Army wagons passed along the road for over half an hour.

> *If you were here it would be a sight for any of you to see. The soldiers are in a continual string as far as you can see with a good proportion of officers. Just a few minutes ago, there was a whole*

*drove of officers passed here, mostly colonels and our General
Cross. They were around viewing the men and works.*[62]

Instead of taking Louisville, Bragg left Bardstown to install
a Confederate governor at Frankfort. Although Union troops
occupied the city, Louisville residents still felt that the Confederates
could attack the city at any moment. Rumors flew around the city
that Smith was at Shelbyville, moving toward Bragg, who was
seven miles northeast of Bardstown. Rumors also circulated that
the Confederacy was about to send another eighty thousand fresh
Confederate troops to Kentucky.

On September 26, 1862, five hundred Confederate cavalrymen
rode into the area of Eighteenth and Oak and captured fifty Union
soldiers. The following night, a Confederate force comprising
one thousand men pushed the Federal pickets back a mile during
a heavy skirmish, which occurred just beyond Middletown on
the Shelbyville Pike. Buell inspected the Home Guard, the men
discharged from hospitals and the refugees and stragglers who were
a large part of Louisville's defense. Many of them carried a musket
for the first time, so Buell ordered a rigid training program.[63]

By September 28, the pontoon bridges over the Ohio were
complete, and troops from Indiana crossed into Louisville. The War
Department ordered Union General William Nelson to command
the newly formed Army of the Ohio. While Louisville prepared
for the Confederate attack by Bragg, Union General Jefferson C.
Davis, who could not reach his command under General Don
Carlos Buell, met with General Nelson to offer his services. General
Nelson gave him the command of the city militia. General Davis
opened an office and went to work assisting in the organization of
the city militia.

General Davis visited General Nelson in his room at the Galt
House and asked Nelson whether the brigade he had been assigned
was ready for service. He also asked if he could obtain arms for them.
General Nelson asked Davis how many men were in his brigade,
and Davis responded that he had about twenty-five hundred men.
General Nelson said angrily, "About twenty-five hundred! About
twenty-five hundred! By God! You a regular officer and come here

to me and report about the number of men in your command? God damn you, don't you know, Sir, you should furnish me the exact number?"

Davis told Nelson that he did not expect to get the guns, but only wanted to learn if he could get them and where. After learning the exact number of troops, he would draw the needed weapons. General Nelson flew into a rage and screamed at General Davis, "About twenty-five hundred! By God I suspend you from your command, and order you to report to General Wright; and I've a damned mind to put you under arrest. Leave my room, Sir!" Davis told General Nelson that he would not leave the room until he gave him an order. General Nelson barked, "The hell you won't! By God I'll put you under arrest, and send you out of the city under a provost guard! Leave my room, Sir!"

General Davis left the room and, in order to avoid arrest, crossed over the river to Jeffersonville, where he remained until the next day, when General Stephen Gano Burbridge joined him. General Burbridge had also been relieved of command by General Nelson under a trivial cause. General Davis went to Cincinnati with General Burbridge and reported to General Wright, who ordered General Davis to return to Louisville and report to General Buell. General Burbridge remained in Cincinnati. General Davis followed Wright's orders.[64]

On September 29, General Nelson ate an early breakfast at the Galt House. After breakfast, he stopped at the hotel desk and inquired whether General Buell, who also had a room on the second floor of the Galt House, had breakfasted yet. The clerk told Nelson that Buell had not eaten. Nelson turned, leaned his back against the counter, faced the people and surveyed the hall. It was then that he noticed General Davis. Davis also saw Nelson, and he asked the governor of Indiana, Oliver Morton, to witness the conversation between him and General Nelson. The governor agreed, and the two walked up to General Nelson.

Davis confronted Nelson and told him that he had taken advantage of his authority. General Nelson sneered and placed a hand to his ear. "Speak louder," he said, "I don't hear very well." Davis, in a louder tone, repeated his statement. Nelson indignantly told Davis that he had not taken advantage of his authority. Davis told Governor Morton that Nelson had threatened to have him arrested and sent out of the state under provost guard. Nelson took his hand and struck Davis twice in the face. "There, damn you, take that!" he bellowed.

Davis started to leave the room, but before going he told Nelson, "This is not the last of it; you will hear from me again." General Nelson turned to Governor Morton and asked him if he had come to insult him, too. Governor Morton stated that he had not come to insult Nelson, but that Davis had requested that he be present and listen to the conversation. General Nelson exclaimed violently to bystanders, "Did you hear the damned rascal insult me?" With that, he walked into the ladies' parlor.

Three minutes later, Davis returned, with a pistol he had borrowed from Captain Gibson of Louisville. He walked toward the door through which Nelson had passed. He saw Nelson walk out of the parlor into the hall separating the main hall from the parlor, and the two faced each other, ten yards apart. General Davis drew his pistol and fired. The ball entered Nelson's heart. General Nelson threw up both hands and grabbed a gentlemen, who stood nearby, around the neck. "I am shot!" he exclaimed.

Nelson walked up the flight of stairs, heading toward General Buell's room, but he sank at the top of the stairs. Fellow officers took General Nelson to his room and laid him on his bed. Nelson requested that Reverend Talbott see him at once. Reverend Talbott administered the ordinance of baptism. The general whispered, "It's all over," and died fifteen minutes later.[65]

News of Nelson's death spread quickly among the regiments. Excited crowds gathered around the Galt House. Rumors circulated that Confederate President Jefferson Davis had snuck into Louisville and shot Nelson. The Union command in Louisville ordered the soldiers back into camp, and a heavy provost guard patrolled the streets. Luckily, Nelson's old command, the Fourth Division, was not in the city when the shooting took place—the members of the division were devoted to Nelson and would have demanded vengeance.

Some of the divisions considered Nelson a tyrant and threw their hats into the air when they heard of his death. J.F. Culver, of

A highly over-dramatized scene of the murder of Union General William "Bull" Nelson by Union General Jefferson C. Davis at the Galt House, October 1, 1862.

the 129th Illinois Infantry, wrote, "General Nelson was killed this morning by General Davis. I have heard no one express any regret. He was disliked by the whole army for being tyrannical, drunken, and very unpleasant."[66] Strangely, the official notice of his death became a terse report in the army's official orders for the day. After his death, Nelson's body lay in state in the Galt House. Later, his body was escorted by twelve hundred men to Christ Church Cathedral and buried in Cave Hill Cemetery.[67] With General Nelson dead, the command switched over to General Don Carlos Buell. Not everyone was happy with Buell taking command of the army. Culver wrote, "Thousands of Buell's men on every side of us proclaim him to be a traitor; that he withheld them when at one stroke he could have destroyed Bragg's entire army."[68]

On September 29, 1862, John Boon wrote to his friends from Louisville that the excitement

> *has somewhat cooled and the citizens have returned to their homes to attend their business...The rush was so great that the people could not cross the boats fast enough so they went to work and built a pontoon bridge to cross on. A pontoon bridge is made by taking large flat boats and anchoring them in the stream and laying timbers across from one boat to the other and then boards on top of the timbers.*

Boon acquired a pass and walked past five houses, tracing the outskirts of the city. He stated that the "houses are all of brick or stone and of fine workmanship. I have seen the house of the Rebel General [Simon] Buckner, one of the best in town."[69] He also mentioned the rainstorm, which filled the streets with mud, and 25 soldiers buried in Louisville. Boon exaggerated the Union troops present in the city and wrote to his friends that Buell had 150,000 men. Although Boon reported that the men were joyful to see friends—laughing, shaking hands and swearing—tempers also flared, and he wrote that two of his officers, a captain and a first lieutenant, had a fight using swords. "The lieutenant was severely used up and it's doubtful if he lives through it. It was a company from Petersburg [Menard County]."[70]

On September 30, Rebel pickets advanced as far as Gilman's Point, present-day St. Matthews, and skirmished with Federal pickets. One of the Federal pickets was killed and one was wounded. A detachment of six thousand to seven thousand Rebels advanced on Gilman's Point. Union infantry, cavalry and artillery "were drawn in line of battle a mile or a mile and a half this side of Middletown awaiting an attack." The Rebel advance forces appeared, and "a charge was made upon them and they were driven back through Middletown as far as Floyd's Fork."[71] Louisville citizens' joy turned to anger and criticism when Buell entered the city on September 25. The citizens complained that Buell should have driven General Edmund Kirby Smith and Braxton Bragg from Kentucky. The soldiers' morale sank as anxiety and rigid training took their toll

Louisville native Captain John Hammond's elaborate presentation sword. Hammond was a member of the Twenty-third Indiana Volunteer Infantry. Because of the neutrality laws in 1861, he had to cross the river to join the Union army.

on the men as they marched and drilled in hot and dry weather. Tempers ran short.[72]

On October 1, 1862, a detachment of Rebel cavalry, under Confederate General Patrick Cleburne's division, drove the Federal pickets "within two or three miles of Louisville, [and] they could hear the 'longroll' beating in every direction."[73]

On October 2, 1862, the Union army marched out of Louisville with sixty thousand men. Bands played, flags fluttered in the wind and the fife and drum corps played music as the soldiers marched out of town. The First Kentucky Infantry began the march at 8:00 a.m., and the streets became clogged with men. The last regiment did not leave the city until 2:00 p.m. Buell sent his three corps along the Shelbyville Pike, the Taylorsville Pike, the Preston Pike and Bardstown Pike. At Fern Creek, Union soldiers overran a Confederate outpost. Thirteen miles out, on the Bardstown Pike, five hundred

Confederate cavalrymen attacked the Sixtieth Indiana Cavalry. In a field, Union soldiers captured four hundred Rebel prisoners and marched them toward Louisville. Union soldiers captured a large part of the Third Georgia Infantry north of Elizabethtown. Buell's advance soldiers pushed Rebel soldiers from New Haven.[74]

While Buell marched his main force toward Bardstown, he sent a small diversionary Federal force to Frankfort to deceive Bragg as to the exact location of the Federal army. The ruse worked. On October 4, 1862, Bragg inaugurated Richard Hawes as the Confederate governor of Kentucky on the statehouse grounds. During the height of the ceremony, General Joshua Sill's small diversionary force shelled Frankfort. Bragg and Confederate Governor Hawes left the city and headed back for Bardstown, thinking the entire Federal force was approaching Frankfort. Bragg decided that all Confederate forces should concentrate at Harrodsburg, Kentucky, ten miles northwest of Danville.[75]

After the Battle of Perryville on October 8, 1862, Louisville city officials prepared for the thousands of wounded Union and Confederate soldiers. City officials appealed for fruit, bandages, socks and medicine. The women of the Louisville Ladies Relief Society labored during the night to be ready for the casualties. Among the workers were Mrs. James Speed, Mrs. Bland Ballard, Mrs. J.H. Heywood, Mrs. Lucy Breckinridge, Mrs. W.B. Belnap, Mrs. Sarah Menefee and Mrs. Hamilton Pope.

On October 10, 1862, General Boyle issued a special order requesting that all furniture wagons, spring wagons and other vehicles suitable for transporting the sick and wounded from the Perryville battlefield to be delivered to Dr. Head, medical director.[76] Hospitals were set up in public schools, homes, factories and churches. The Fifth Ward School, built at Fifth and York Streets in 1855, became Military Hospital Number Eight. The United States Marine Hospital also became a hospital for the wounded Union soldiers from the Battle of Perryville. Constructed between 1845 and 1852, the three-story, Greek revival–style Louisville Marine Hospital contained one hundred beds and became the prototype for seven U.S. Marine Hospital Service buildings, including Paducah, Kentucky, which later became Fort Anderson. Union surgeons

The U.S. Marine Hospital, located on Portland Avenue, was built in 1837. The hospital was closed to boatmen in 1863 and became a military hospital for the duration of the war.

erected the Brown General Hospital, located near the Belnap campus of the University of Louisville, and other hospitals were erected at Jeffersonville and New Albany, Indiana.

Jeffersonville had one of the best hospitals. The hospital covered 117 acres at a cost of $250,000 dollars, with two thousand beds, which later increased to twenty-six hundred beds. The hospital was shaped like a huge wheel, with a circular corridor, 80 feet wide in diameter, and twenty wards, each 32 feet wide and 175 feet long. Each ward had a dining room, pantry, ward master's room, bathroom, washroom, water pipes, ventilation apparatus, gas lights and offices. Dr. Middleton Goldsmith was chief surgeon.[77] Fifty surgeons and 272 nurses cared for the wounded, but the city still needed more qualified physicians to care for the endless injured that poured into the city. By October 29, 1,050 wounded soldiers arrived in the city. By February 1863, Louisville had nineteen hospitals, with another hospital in Jeffersonville and eight in New Albany.

Casualty lists appeared in the *Louisville Journal* reporting on the killed and wounded from the Fifteenth Kentucky and Stone's battery, also known as the Louisville Battery A, First Kentucky Volunteer Regiment Artillery. In the Fifteenth Kentucky, Lieutenant Colonel George Jouett, Major Campbell and Lieutenant McGrath of Company B, were killed. Colonel Pope was wounded and later died from typhoid fever on November 5, 1862. Lieutenant McClure of the Fifteenth Kentucky was also wounded. On October 15, funeral services were held at Chestnut Presbyterian Church for Lieutenant Colonel Jouett and Major Campbell, and one of the largest processions ever seen in Louisville followed the caskets to Cave Hill Cemetery.[78]

The colors of the Fifteenth Kentucky were shot down during the Battle of Perryville, and the color sergeant was severely wounded. He was rescued by and taken from the field by Captain James Brown Foreman. The ladies of Louisville made another flag for the Fifteenth Kentucky and presented the flag to Captain Foreman, who later was commissioned colonel and led the regiment to Nashville. The old bullet-ridden and torn flag from the Fifteenth Kentucky was given to the state for preservation. In Captain David C. Stone's battery, Sergeant Jacob Kennett and Corporal William Voskhule were killed, and Edward Dowden was mortally wounded, along with ten other wounded men.

After the battle, the remains of General James Jackson, General William Terrill and General George Webster arrived in the city. General Terrill's and General Webster's bodies awaited the orders of their friends. Mrs. Terrill, the widow of General Terrill, was in Cincinnati when she heard of her husband's death. Mrs. Terrill shipped her husband's remains home. The remains of General James Jackson were embalmed and laid in state at the Galt House, then taken to Christ Church Cathedral, where a large congregation assembled to participate in the funeral rites. Captain Starling, Captain Oldershaw, Captain S. Fillitler, Adjutant General Finnell, Zeb Ward, Gibson Mallory, William Milton, former Governor Charles Wickliffe and others served as pallbearers and acted as escorts. The funeral cortege was composed of the Twenty-fifth Michigan Cavalry, a detachment of the Fourth Indiana Cavalry and a long line of mourning friends. The funeral services were conducted by Reverend H.H. Talbott. General Jackson's family later took his remains to Christian County for final interment.

On October 13, 130 prisoners arrived from the Battle of Perryville. One of the prisoners, T.M. Blair, came from the famous Washington Artillery, Fifth Company, from New Orleans. The Louisville Legion, under the command of Major Jack Trainor, escorted the prisoners to the Union Army Prison, also called the "Louisville Military Prison." The Louisville Military Prison took over the old Medical College building at the corner of Green and Fifth Streets. Union authorities later moved the prison near the corner of Tenth and Broadway. The prison had a capacity of 300 men. From October 1, 1862, to December 14, 1862, the new Louisville Military Prison housed 3,504 prisoners. In December 1863, over 2,000 prisoners, including political prisoners, Federal deserters and Confederate prisoners of war, were located in the military prison.

The prison was made of wood and covered an entire city block, stretching from east and west between Tenth and Eleventh Streets and north and south by Magazine Street and Broadway. The main entrance to the prison was located on Broadway near Tenth Street. A high fence surrounded the prison with at least two prison barracks. The prison hospital was attached to the prison and consisted of two barracks on the south and west sides of the square, with forty beds in each building. The Union commander at the Louisville Military Prison was Colonel Dent, but in April 1863, military authorities replaced him with Captain Stephen E. Jones. In October 1863, military authorities replaced Captain Jones with C.B. Pratt.[79]

Just a block away from the Louisville Military Prison, Union authorities took over a large house on Broadway between Twelfth and Thirteenth Streets and converted the house into a female military prison.

Chapter 6

Louisville Begins to Change

On January 1, 1863, President Abraham Lincoln passed the Emancipation Proclamation, which stated that all slaves in the rebellion states would be freed. Louisville rose up against the Proclamation. With the passage of the Emancipation Proclamation and the recruitment of slaves into the Union army, and with thousands of Union soldiers inhabiting their city, bringing with them crime and gambling, Louisville began to openly support the Confederacy. Two paroled Confederate soldiers in Louisville, Marcus Toney and Captain Merritt S. Pilcher, wore their gray uniforms in the streets of Louisville and attended the Walnut Street Baptist Church and Christ Church Cathedral in their uniforms. Citizens stopped them on the street to shake their hands. A Federal soldier visited a ball given at the home of W.W. Owen. When he entered the residence, he noticed that a number of guests wore gray and that the party was in honor of a number of paroled Confederate soldiers. At the end of night, the Union soldier was shocked when the guests sang "Bonnie Blue Flag." The provost marshal raided the residence and arrested twenty-two guests.[80]

Louisville formed a subversive organization known as the "Star Organization," which had links to the Copperhead movement, the American Knights and the Sons of Liberty. Dr. Henry Kalfus, a former member of the Fifteenth Kentucky Union Infantry, had an office opposite the jail on Jefferson Street, between Sixth and Seventh, that doubled as a meeting place for the Knights of the

Golden Circle. The home of Mrs. Jack Taylor, at 519 First Street, was used as a meeting place for the Knights. So was the home of Anna Thompson, the daughter of W.T. Thompson. The Knights encouraged Union soldier desertion, harboring deserters, giving intelligence to the Confederates and smuggling ammunition to the South.

On April 5, William Kaye became the mayor of Louisville. On April 13, 1863, Union General Ambrose Burnside became the new commander of the Department of the Ohio, including Kentucky. Burnside's Order Number 38 declared that sending and receiving secret mails were punishable by death. People declaring sympathy with the Confederacy would be arrested and tried as traitors, and if convicted, they suffered death or were sent beyond Union lines.[81]

On May 21, 1863, Union soldiers destroyed the fairgrounds, and the owner sold the property for $15,600 dollars. The new owner opened the new fairgrounds in time for the Kentucky State Fair in September. Soldiers also destroyed the beautifully landscaped grounds at Cave Hill Cemetery by cutting rifle pits through the graves and allowing the flowers and shrubs to be eaten by the Union cows, which were allowed to roam the cemetery.[82]

With thousands of soldiers arriving in Louisville, gambling became a huge business in the city. All of the north side of Jefferson, from Fourth Street to the east side of Fifth Street, from Jefferson to Market and from the south side of Market from Fifth to Fourth, was devoted to keno, faro, roulette and poker.[83] Drunken soldiers jammed the saloons. Many of the soldiers felt that Louisville was in Rebel territory, and they treated the citizens accordingly. Gamblers, conmen, saloon keepers and women of ill repute victimized the soldiers.

Chapter 7

Morgan's 1863 Raid and Guerilla Warfare

During Confederate General John Hunt Morgan's Great Raid in July 1863, he attacked the Green River Bridge and Lebanon. His cavalry headed straight for Louisville, but Morgan was smart enough not to take on the fortified city. Instead, he took Brandenburg and captured two steamboats, which ferried his men across the river into Indiana. Morgan sent a diversionary force east of Louisville. He ordered William Davis of Company D, Second Kentucky, and Company A, Eighth Kentucky, to cut the telegraph lines, burn railroad bridges and create the impression that his two companies were actually Morgan's entire force. Davis's force was to take Twelve Mile Island above Louisville, cross the Ohio and rejoin Morgan's men at Salem, Indiana. On July 11, Davis's force attempted to cross the river at Twelve Mile Island, but the gunboat *Moose* turned them back. Union General Mahlon Manson arrived with a large force in ten steamboats and captured most of Davis's men.

On February 4, 1864, an important meeting took place at the Galt House. Union Generals Ulysses S. Grant, William S. Rosecrans, George Stoneman, Thomas Crittenden, James Wadsworth, David Hunter, John Schofield, Alexander McCook, Robert Allen, George Thomas, Stephen Burbridge and Rear Admiral David Porter met to discuss the most important campaign of the war, which would eventually rip the Confederacy into three parts.

On February 14, 1864, Major General Ulysses S. Grant ordered Brigadier General Stephen Gano Burbridge to Camp Nelson,

Kentucky native Union General Stephen Gano Burbrigde, district commander in 1864, had his headquarters in Louisville.

located in southern Jessamine County, Kentucky, to command the District of Kentucky until relieved by General Jacob Ammen, who was on court-martial duty. On January 12, 1864, Union authorities relieved General Jeremiah Boyle of command. Burbridge would report to Grant for an assignment. By Order Number 41, Burbridge was assigned to command the District of Kentucky.[84]

On February 22, 1864, Cave Hill Cemetery laid the cornerstone for the soldiers monuments in the Union section of the cemetery.

On March 4, all barrooms, groceries, confectionaries and other retail liquor houses in Louisville, Jeffersonville and Portland were closed until the owners offered evidence that they did not sell liquor to the soldiers.

On March 9, 1864, Grant met Union General William T. Sherman at the Galt House and discussed the spring campaign. Grant would take on Confederate General Robert E. Lee and take

Richmond, while Sherman took on Confederate General Joseph E. Johnston and took Atlanta.[85]

Eventually, 24,438 slaves enlisted in the Union army and received their freedom upon joining. The Taylor Barracks, on Third and Oak Street in Louisville, was the induction point for Kentucky black recruits. Since black soldiers could not stay in white soldiers' hospitals, the military built the Hospital d'Afrique in New Albany, Indiana. The black Union soldiers who died from disease were not buried in Cave Hill Cemetery; rather, they were interred in Louisville's Eastern Cemetery.[86]

On July 1, 1864, a huge fire broke out in the city of Louisville that consumed an entire block between Water and Main and Eighth and Ninth Streets. The government lost $800,000.

On July 16, Burbridge issued Order Number 59, which stated that a rapid increase in his district of lawless bands of armed men engaged in interrupting railroad and telegraphic communications, plundering and murdering peaceful Union citizens, destroying the mails, et cetera, called for the adoption of stringent measures by the military for their suppression. In his order, he stated that all guerillas, armed prowlers (or by whatever name they were known) and Rebel sympathizers were warned and that, in the future, stern retaliatory measures would be adopted and strictly enforced whenever the lives or property of peaceful citizens were jeopardized by the lawless acts of such men. He wrote that any Rebel sympathizers living within five miles of any scene of outrage committed by armed men, who were not recognized as public enemies by the rules and usages of war, would be arrested and sent beyond the limited of the United States. The property of Rebel sympathizers would be used to repay the government or loyal citizens for losses incurred by the acts of lawless men, or would be seized and appropriated to those who had lost property.

Burbridge stated that whenever an unarmed Union citizen was murdered, four guerillas would be selected from the prisoners in the hands of the military authorities and publicly shot to death in the most convenient place near the scene of outrage.[87] The *Louisville Daily Journal* published his Order Number 59 on July 20, 1864, and added that the murder of Union men would be avenged. The paper asked that the guerilla bands lay down their arms and quietly return to the "peaceable pursuits of life." The paper also stated that the guerilla bands have "trampled all laws under their feet and erased all forms that might grant to them a show of trial." According to the paper, General Burbridge's order "falls like a stream of golden sunshine upon the dark storm clouds of an angry sky."[88]

Unfortunately, General Burbridge's Order Number 59 caused Confederate prisoners to be mistaken for outlaws, and many innocent men paid with their lives. The evidence against many of the Rebels or guerillas was very often flimsy. With a few choice words of criticism against a Federal officer, the report that a son or brother in the Confederate army had returned home or the personal grudge of some Unionist against one of his enemies, Burbridge was authorized to arrest, imprison and confiscate property.[89] The reign of terror had begun, and Burbridge did not take long to implement his Order Number 59.

On July 22, 1864, six days after Burbridge issued his Order Number 59, the military authorities took two young men named John Pierman Powell, age twenty-three, and Charles William Thompson, age eighteen, from the military prison in Louisville to Henderson, Kentucky, to be executed under Order Number 59. Union commander Lieutenant Headington had orders to execute the two young men for the "atrocious attempt of a gang of guerilla scoundrels and marauders...to murder in cold blood, Mr. Jas. E. Rankin...and for other outrages of late in Henderson and vicinity."[90] Both Powell and Thompson were Confederate soldiers who had been captured on July 12, 1864, about five miles from Owensboro. The two young men claimed they were members of a company commanded by Confederate Captain Dick Yates, a commissioned officer who was killed in a skirmish near Owensboro. Originally on a recruiting mission, Captain Yates and the two young men met some Federal soldiers and some one hundred Home Guards on Ruff Creek, killing eleven and routing the rest. Thompson and Powell unfortunately became separated from the rest of the company and were captured by the Union forces. On July 20, Union soldiers moved the two men to the Henderson County Jail to await their execution.[91]

The reason for Powell and Thompson's order for execution stemmed from an incident that occurred on July 11, 1864, in Henderson. A band of outlaws looted the establishment of Mr. James Rankin of Henderson. The leader of the group ordered the robbers to leave. Rankin hid in a back room on the third floor. The leader returned with a group of other men and found Mr. Rankin. They demanded that he open the safe, but Rankin told the men he did not have all the pieces to assemble the combination key. As Mr. Rankin descended the stairs to see if he could find the pieces for the lock, one of the outlaws shot him in the back of his neck and beat him with the butt of his gun. Rankin ran to a nearby store. The outlaws chased him into another store. William Lewis, a store clerk, begged for Mr. Rankin's life. The outlaws turned and left.[92]

Although severely wounded, Mr. Rankin refused to receive any part of the $18,000 dollars forcibly collected from his neighbors to pay him his losses by guerillas.[93] Mr. Rankin sent a note requesting that Lieutenant Headington spare the two young men. Two prominent citizens from Henderson, Archibald Dixon and Mayor Banks, sent a telegram to Union General Hugh Ewing requesting a stay of execution because the citizens of the town feared retribution from the outlaws, and the two young men claimed they were not robbers but sworn Confederate soldiers. General Ewing agreed to delay the execution until he spoke with General Burbridge. On July 20, 1864, the steamer *Palestine* transported Thompson and Powell from the Henderson County Jail to the site of their execution.

On July 22, Colonel Headington received orders from Burbridge to proceed with the execution, but not for the attack on Rankin but for the murder of Colonel James Poole. Both Powell and Thompson were placed in chairs with their arms fastened to fence boards. Union soldiers blindfolded them. Colonel Headington shed tears before giving the command to fire.[94] Twelve Union soldiers fired a volley into the body of Powell and then into Thompson. After the execution, Headington handed over both bodies to the local citizens, who cleaned them and sent them to their friends in Curdsville, Daviess County, Kentucky. After arriving in Daviess County, Powell and Thompson were laid to rest in double graves at the St. Alfonsus Parish Catholic Cemetery at St. Joseph's Church. In the later part of July, James Rankin died of his wounds.

On July 27, Union General James McPherson's body arrived on the early morning train and was taken to the Galt House. General McPherson was killed during the Battle of Atlanta. At 11:00 a.m., the funeral procession formed, with a long line of cavalry and infantry. McPherson's body was taken from the chamber and carried to the elegant black-plumed hearse. The Union flag was folded around the general's coffin. His sword was sheathed and laid upon the bier. The coffin was carried down the steps and loaded into the hearse. The procession moved down Main Street, between Second and Third Streets. The advance was led by a platoon of cavalry, followed by the band playing a "low, dirge-like music." A column of infantry was next, followed by the plumed hearse, with Generals Hugh Ewing and Robert Allen as two of the pallbearers. The hearse was guarded by another infantry battalion, followed by yet another battalion of infantry and the personal escort of the general. Leaning upon the arm of the senior staff officers was General McPherson's brother, wearing a civilian suit of plain black. Closing upon the escort's rear came the various officers on duty in the city. A mounted platoon, followed by the Ninth Pennsylvania Cavalry on foot, brought up the rear of the military. Then came the citizens on foot.

As the procession advanced to the mail boat landing, the cannon, at stated intervals, thundered a salute in McPherson's honor. As the head of the procession began to form in parade line on the levee, the rear was just leaving the Galt House. The flags throughout the city and on the steamboats were at half-mast. The coffin was removed from the hearse and carried onboard the steamboat, with sad, wailing music "falling in mournful cadences in the presence of heads bowed in respect and the parade line at present arms." The troops in the procession were the Ninth Pennsylvania and the Twenty-sixth Kentucky Infantry. Fifty-two men of the Thirteenth U.S. Infantry were detailed by General Sherman to accompany the body to Ohio for final interment.[95]

On July 28, 1864, Union spy Felix Stidger, in Indianapolis, learned that a day had been set for an armed uprising by the Sons of Liberty. Alarmed by the news, Stidger met with Union General Henry Carrington, Governor Oliver Morton of Indiana, Governor Thomas Bramlette, Burbridge and Colonel Fairleigh. Stidger told the assembly that fifteen hundred trained and well-armed men were ready to attack Camp Morton at Indianapolis and free six thousand Confederate prisoners. He also reminded them that the nearby state and Federal arsenals had enough arms to equip six thousand men. In Kentucky, Stidger told the council, a band of members was waiting for the signal to set the whole city of Louisville on fire. Seven regiments of seasoned Confederate soldiers were hiding their arms, waiting to assemble on the day of the uprising.[96]

On July 29, two alleged guerillas were sent from the prison in Louisville to Russellville, Logan County, to be shot on the spot where Mr. Porter died from wounds while resisting the outrages of guerillas. Union soldiers chose only Harvey Thomas of Company C, Second Kentucky Cavalry, a twenty-three-year-old from Williamson County, Tennessee, to be executed. Union soldiers ordered the stores in Russellville closed and for the businesses owners to be present for the execution. At sundown, twelve soldiers from Captain Page's Company E, Twenty-sixth Kentucky Infantry, fired six bullets into the body of Harvey Thomas.[97]

On July 30, 1864, Burbridge acted on information he had gathered on a secret conspiracy in Kentucky. He ordered the arrest of the leading members in Louisville, who belonged to the Sons of Liberty. Burbridge also ordered the arrest of Chief Justice for the State of Kentucky Joshua Bullitt. As the ferry between Jeffersonville, Indiana and Louisville prepared to leave the wharf, Federal agents arrested Bullitt. During the next two weeks, military authorities arrested Dr. Henry F. Kalfus, W.K. Thomas, Alfred Harris, G.S.G. Payne, Joseph R. Buchanan, Thomas Jeffries, J.J. Paul, John Hines, John Colgan, Henry Stickrod, Michael Carroll, William Fitzhenry, Erwin Bell, A.J. Brannon, Thomas Miller, A.J. Mitchell, John Rudd, Charles J. Clarke, B.C. Redford, John H. Talbott and W.G. Gray, all of whom were residents of Jefferson County and Louisville.

The next day, Secretary of War Edwin Stanton wrote to Burbridge that his actions against the disloyal persons in his command were approved. He also authorized Burbridge to establish his headquarters in Louisville. He could reenlist all the cavalry he could mount for general service for one year. General Ulysses S. Grant suggested that the new organizations, white and black, should be enlisted as infantry and mounted. His mode of mounting cavalry by seizing horses from disloyal citizens was approved, and he authorized Burbridge to seize all the horses he could lay his hands on. Grant also placed the State of Kentucky under Burbridge's order.

On August 10, 1864, the *Louisville Democrat* reported that "a large number of political prisoners are confined in the military barracks here, and the number is being increased daily by the arrival of prisoners arrested in other portions of the state."

During the months of July and August, Burbridge set out to build more fortifications in Kentucky. As Sherman marched through Georgia, Kentucky no longer faced a threat from the Confederate army, but Burbridge felt the need to build earthworks. He received permission from Union General John Schofield to build fortifications in Mount Sterling, Lexington, Frankfort and Louisville. The plans called for each location to have a small, enclosed fieldwork of about two hundred yards along the interior crest, with the exception of Louisville, which would be five hundred yards. Other earthworks would follow in Louisville as opportunity and the means available allowed. All the works were to be built by soldiers, except at Frankfort, where the works were constructed by the state and at Louisville, where they were done by the city. Lieutenant Colonel J. H. Simpson, of the Federal Engineers, furnished the plans and engineering force.

Eleven forts protected the city in a ring about ten miles long from Beargrass Creek to Paddy's Run. They included, from east to west: Fort Elstner, between Frankfort Avenue and Brownsboro Road, near Bellaire, Vernon and Emerald Avenues; Fort Engle, at Spring Street and Arlington Avenue; Fort Saunders, at Cave Hill Cemetery; Battery Camp Fort Hill, between Goddard Avenue, Barrett and Baxter Streets and St. Louis Cemetery; Fort Horton, at Shelby and Merriweather Streets (present-day incinerator plant); Fort McPherson, on Preston Street, bounded by Barbee, Brandis, Hahn and Fort Streets; Fort Philpot, at Seventh Street and Algonquin Parkway; Fort St. Clair Morton, at Sixteenth and

The headstone for Kentucky Governor Thomas Bramlette, located at Cave Hill Cemetery. Elected as governor on the Union Democratic ticket in 1863, Bramlette was a friend of Union General Stephen Burbridge, district commander for the State of Kentucky. Bramlette turned against him when Burbridge recruited and armed slaves for the Union army.

Hill Streets; Fort Karnasch, on Wilson Avenue between Twenty-sixth and Twenty-eighth Streets; Fort Clark, at Thirty-sixth and Magnolia Streets; Battery Gallup, at Gibson Lane and Forty-third Street; and Fort Southworth, on Paddy's Run at the Ohio River (now the site of a city sewage treatment plant with a marker located at 4522 Algonquin Parkway).

Also in the area was Camp Gilbert and Camp C.F. Smith, although the exact locations of both sites have been lost to history. The first work built was Fort McPherson, which commanded the approaches to the city via the Shepherdsville Pike, Third Street Road and the Louisville and Nashville Railroad. The fort served as a citadel if an attack came before the other forts were completed. The fort could house one thousand men. General Hugh Ewing, Union commander in Louisville, directed that municipal authorities furnish laborers for fortifications, ordered the arrest of all "loafers found about gambling and other disreputable establishments" in

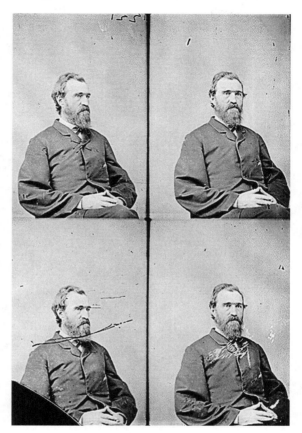

Governor Thomas Bramlette. *Courtesy of the National Archives.*

the city for construction work and assigned military convicts to the work. Each fort was a basic earth and timber structure surrounded by a ditch, with a movable drawbridge at the entrance to the fort, and each was furnished with an underground magazine to house two hundred rounds of artillery shells. The eleven forts occupied the most commanding positions to provide interlocking crossfire between them. A supply of entrenching tools was collected and stored for emergency construction of additional batteries and infantry entrenchments between the fortifications. The guns in the Louisville forts never fired, except for salutes.[98]

On August 20, 1864, Brigadier General Hugh Ewing ordered

A historical marker discussing Fort Southworth, located at 4522 Algonquin Parkway.

the post commander in Louisville to select four guerillas and send them to Franklin, Kentucky, to be publicly shot for the murder of Union men. Union soldiers only took three men to Franklin. They executed J. Bloom and W.B. McGlassin for the death of Mr. Harvey Travelated, a Union citizen of Simpson County, Kentucky, who was shot and killed by "the notorious scoundrel Harper."[99]

On September 2, 1864, Burbridge heard about the murder of Mr. David Henry of Meade County, Kentucky. He ordered Union Lieutenant Colonel Fairleigh, post commander at Louisville, to select four guerillas from Thomas Dupoyster's men and send them

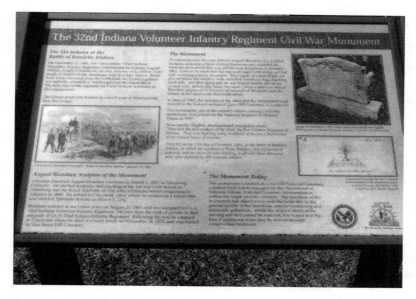

The Thirty-second Indiana's monument at Cave Hill Cemetery. The monument is the oldest known Civil War monument.

to Brandenburg to be publicly shot in retaliation for the murder of David Henry. Union Lieutenant Colonel Fairleigh took John Brooks, of Jackson, Mississippi; Robert Blinco, of Hawesville; Frank Holmes, of Cloverport; and Julius Bradis, of Louisville, to Brandenburg. All the prisoners were regular Confederate soldiers. Brandis stated that he was a soldier from Company L, Second Kentucky Cavalry. Confederate Captain Rolla sought recruits for his command and enlisted Frank Holmes into his small band of twenty-five men. Lieutenant John Brooks belonged to the Eighth Kentucky Infantry, Company A, then the Tenth Kentucky Partisan Rangers, Company C, and later made captain in the Sixteenth Kentucky Cavalry in August 1864. The prisoners were unlucky to draw black beans from a box containing hundreds of white beans.[100]

A resident of Meade County, David Henry was an ardent Union supporter and prominent farmer. A guerilla leader known only as Captain Bryant and seven of his men arrived at Henry's home in late August 1864 and demanded to be fed dinner and given feed for their horses. As they rode away, Henry shot at the guerillas and shouted for a Union lieutenant to flank the guerillas from the rear. Bryant and his men thought that the Yankee cavalry was hot on their trail and headed for safety. Later, Captain Bryant realized he had been tricked. There was no Union cavalry in the area, and he swore revenge upon Henry. On August 28, 1864, Captain John Bryant and thirty-five men surrounded Henry's house and demanded that he come out. Henry, who hid upstairs, heard his daughter pleading with the guerillas to spare her father's life. After a while, Henry decided to head downstairs, while Bryant waited on the back porch. When Henry came within range of Bryant's pistol, Bryant fired and killed him.

When the prisoners arrived at Brandenburg, Lieutenant John Enoch of the Fifty-fourth Ohio Infantry took charge and escorted them to the Henry Farm. George Prentice, editor of the *Louisville Journal*, described the four young, unmarried men as having received "many advantages in younger days."[101] The pastor of the Brandenburg Baptist Church, George H. Hicks, accompanied the four men to the Henry Farm. At 2:00 p.m. on September 4, 1864, the four men knelt and thanked their captors for their gentle kindness. Twenty Union soldiers were divided into four squads of five men each, with each squad having a gun loaded with a blank. Each prisoner folded his hands across his chest and kept his eyes closed. As the shots rang out, each man fell to the ground without a groan.[102] Four more men lost their lives to Order Number 59. After the execution, the bodies were placed in a wagon and taken back to Brandenburg. The citizens volunteered to take care of the bodies and preserve them for the friends of the deceased. Lieutenant Enoch accepted their offer and took his men aboard a steamer headed back to Louisville.[103]

On October 25, in retaliation for the shooting of a Union soldier by Confederate guerrilla Sue Munday's men near Brunerstown, present-day Jeffersontown, Jefferson County, Wilson Lilly, a member of Company G, First Missouri Volunteer Infantry; Sherwood Hatley, a seventy-year-old Presbyterian minister; Lindsey Duke Buckner, a Confederate captain in Colonel Chenoweth's regiment;

and William Blincoe, a member of Company D, Second Kentucky Cavalry, were taken from a military prison by Captain Rowland E. Hackett and fifty Union soldiers of the Twenty-sixth Kentucky Union Infantry and escorted to the spot where the Federal soldier was killed. All four men were shot by Captain Hackett and his men.[104] While seated on his coffin, awaiting execution, Captain Lindsey Buckner wrote a farewell letter to his sister, Mrs. Louisa J. Edwards. Lindsey wrote that he was

> *under sentence of death and for what, I do not know. My sentence is not yet made known. My dear sister, I have always loved you and will in my dying breath. It is a hard thing to be chained and shot in this way; and if it was not for the hope I have of meeting you all in Heaven, I would be miserable indeed.*[105]

The next day, Colonel Sam Johnson, commander of the Forty-eighth Kentucky Infantry, took Lieutenant Colonel James Brewer, a volunteer aide de camp to John C. Breckinridge, and Private Thomas Bassett, Company K, First Kentucky Cavalry, to be executed in Hopkinsville, Kentucky. Colonel Johnson had been a Methodist preacher in Logan County, but he quit the pulpit to join the Union army. He hated Southern soldiers and sympathizers. When Johnson's men brought Brewer in as a prisoner, the Union soldiers asked Johnson what to do with him. He exclaimed, "By God, get a squad and take him down to the river bank and shoot him…Go down to the jail and get that d—ed fellow Bassett and shoot him too." The Union soldiers directed both Brewer and Bassett to kneel with their backs to the squad. Bassett turned his back sobbing. Brewer stood erect and said, "I never turn my back to the enemy. I only ask that you do not shoot me in the face." Colonel Johnson sat on his horse nearby while his men shot and killed both men.[106]

On November 8, 1864, two Rebels named Richard Cheney and J. Peters, McDonald or Jones were taken from the military prison in Louisville and shot at Munfordville in Hart County in retaliation for the murder of James Madison Murphy, Company A, Thirteenth Kentucky Infantry, by guerrillas. According to the provost marshal of Munfordville, twenty or thirty men dressed in civilian clothing came to the house of David Cavin on the Green River and took Murphy out of bed, hauled him into the woods near Murphy's brother's (Benjamin Murphy) house, shot him in the head and threw him into the sinkhole in the woods. The next day, two blacks were killed, and Burbridge selected James Hopkins, John W. Sipple and Samuel Stagdale to be shot at Bloomfield in Nelson County, Kentucky.[107]

Also on November 8, 1864, Lincoln was reelected president of the United States. Although Burbridge tried to influence the election by getting Lincoln elected in Kentucky, Union General George B. McClellan received 61,486 votes, while Lincoln only received 26,592. Lincoln received majorities in 25 counties out of the 101 reporting, and in 56 counties he received over 100 votes. In only 8 counties did McClellan receive over 100 votes. Historian E. Merton Coulter stated that there were 54,000 fewer votes cast in the 1864 election than in 1860, which indicated the great demoralization that prevailed in the state. He wrote:

Although military interference was not nearly so glaring as it had been in previous elections, still some of the falling off must be attributed to intimidation by the army, for [Robert] *Breckinridge and* [General Stephen] *Burbridge sedulously worked to create the impression that the test of loyalty, which meant payment for slaves and property seized and freedom from arrest and persecution, would be determined by the way a person voted—if he voted at all. And many, doubtless, considered no record better than a bad one—hence they stayed at home.*[108]

Chapter 8

How Terrible the Calamity!

On January 10, 1865, at 1:00 a.m., a fire started in the Galt House, and by 2:30 a.m. the entire hotel was in flames. The fire spread rapidly, and the four-story building next door also went up in flames. Two corpses were found in the ruins. The loss of the Galt House amounted to $557,000 in damages. Guests staying at the Galt House lost $100,000 dollars in the fire. Since the beginning of the Civil War, almost every single Union general in the Western theater had stayed in the glamorous hotel. The Galt House, which saw the murder of Union General William Buell Nelson and the most important meeting of the Civil War between Grant and Sherman, now lay in ruins.

On January 20, 1865, Nathaniel Marks, formerly of Company A, Fourth Kentucky, was condemned as a guerilla. He claimed he was innocent but was shot by a firing squad in Louisville.

On January 24, a group of Union soldiers shot a citizen in Portland. After the shooting, the soldiers began to loot the stores. Along the entire length of Portland Avenue, the soldiers continued to loot the stores and saloons. Soldiers robbed and shot two local citizens. The city sent out the local police, and the military sent a force of three hundred infantrymen and cavalrymen to patrol the streets, day and night. The guards had orders to shoot down any soldier caught in the act of a misdemeanor.[109]

On January 27, the military prison at Fifth and Green Streets burned. Only thirty Confederate prisoners of war remained in the prison, and one prisoner died in the fire.

THE GALT HOUSE

A world-famed inn operated here from 1835 until it burned in 1865. Host to notables, such as author Charles Dickens, it was scene of assassination of USA Gen. Wm. Nelson, Sept. 1862, by USA Gen. J. C. Davis. Sherman and Grant met here March, 1864 to plan invasion that led to the "March to the Sea." Traditions carried on at new Galt House at 1st and Main, 1869-1921.

A historical marker on Second Street, discussing the original site of the Galt House, which burned toward the end of the Civil War.

On February 10, 1865, Burbridge's term as military governor came to an end. Secretary of War Edwin Stanton replaced Burbridge with Major General John Palmer.

On March 1, 1865, guerillas entered Louisville, helped themselves to Julius Fosses, who was the assistant inspector general of cavalry, and two elegant horses valued at $2,000 and rode out of the city.

On March 7, 1865, General Palmer continued Burbridge's black policies; he ordered all the slave pens suppressed and freed all the confined slaves. He asked that all white troops be released from guard duty in the city to defend the state against guerillas, and he placed black soldiers on guard and local duty, to the consternation of the citizens.[110]

On March 9, 1865, following a skirmish at Howard's Mill, Kentucky, Union authorities sent Union troops to Owingsville to chase several bands of guerillas. On March 12, fifty Union soldiers from the Thirtieth Wisconsin Infantry, under the command of Major Cyrus Wilson, surrounded a tobacco barn ten miles south of Brandenburg forces near Breckinridge County. At daybreak, the

Union soldiers fired into the barn. Gunfire erupted from the barn, and four Union soldiers fell wounded. Inside the barn were the famous guerillas Jerome Clarke (a.k.a. Sue Mundy), Henry Medkiff and Henry Magruder. Major Wilson had earlier injured Magruder at Howard's Mill. Major Wilson told Clarke that his men would be treated as prisoners of war if he surrendered. Clarke agreed, and Major Wilson escorted all three men to Brandenburg, where they boarded a steamer for Louisville. Military authorities kept Clarke's trial a secret, and the verdict had already been decided the day before the trial.

On March 14, military authorities planned Clarke's execution, even though the trial had not even started. At the brief hearing, Clarke "stood firm and spoke with perfect composure." He stated that he was a regular Confederate soldier and that he had not committed the crimes with which he was being charged; they had been committed by William Quantrill. During the three-hour trial, Clarke was not allowed counsel or witnesses for his defense. Three days after his capture, Union authorities scheduled Clarke for public hanging just west of the corner of Eighteenth and Broadway in Louisville.

By April, the General Hospitals that remained in Louisville were the office of D.H. Gilbert, surgeon, U.S. Volunteers, and superintendent and medical director, U.S. General Hospitals for Louisville and Jeffersonville, located on Walnut, between Fourth and Fifth Streets; Officers U.S. General Hospital, on the corner of Brook and Broadway; Brown U.S. General Hospital, on the hill east of Park Barracks on Third Street; Crittenden General Hospital, on the corner of Fifteenth Street and Broadway; Clay General Hospital, on Sixth Street between Walnut and Chestnut; Eruptive Hospital (for smallpox and measles), on Newburg Road, three miles from the city; Foundry General Hospital, on the corner of Fifteenth and Main Streets; Sedgewick General Hospital, on the corner of Fifteenth and Broadway; Strader General Hospital, at the foot of Fourth Street; and Transfer General Hospital, at Broadway near the Nashville Depot.

In Jeffersonville, the Jeffersonville General Hospital was located one mile east of the city; Joe Holt General Hospital was one

Seven wards of the Crittenden Hospital on the northeast corner of Fifteenth and Broadway. *Courtesy of the National Archives.*

mile west of the city; and No. 16 General Hospital was near the railroad depot. In New Albany, Indiana, the medical director of the Northern Department in charge of the General Hospitals was Charles Tripler. Hospital No. 4 was located on the upper corner Ninth and Main; Hospital No. 5 (for black soldiers) was located on the northwest corner of Main and Lafayette; Hospital No. 6, on Elm Street, between upper Sixth and Seventh; Hospital No. 8, on Main Street, between Pearl and Slate Street; and the Floating Hospital *Ohio* (black Union soldiers), at the foot of lower Fourth Street.

On April 14, to celebrate the surrender of General Robert E. Lee, Mayor Kaye ordered the Louisville Fire Department, the city council, the city officers and all the citizens of Louisville to join in a procession from Jefferson Street to Fifteenth Street, down Fifteenth Street to Market Street, up Market to Eleventh Street, down Eleventh to Main Street, up Main to Jackson Street, out Jackson to Walnut Street, down Walnut to Preston Street, out Preston to Chestnut, down Chestnut to Eighth Street, out Eighth to Broadway, up Broadway to Second Street, down Second to Walnut, down Walnut to Fourth Street, down Fourth to Jefferson and down Jefferson back to the beginning. The procession would take place at night in order to illuminate the city.

The procession was a mile long. The sidewalks on both sides of Jefferson Street were jammed with spectators. The steam engines from the fire department were decorated with flags and inscriptions. The Twentieth Wisconsin Infantry added to the grandeur. Many

New barracks on Broadway, west of Crittenden Hospital (far right). Fifteenth Street was cut through the entrenchments. *Courtesy of the National Archives.*

of the businesses were closed. Market Street was illuminated from one end to the other. The medical storekeepers' office had banners with the inscription: "The Medical Department—Drs. Grant, Sherman, and Sheridan—prescribed bitter pills for the Rebels." A large number of the prominent businesses on Main Street were lighted up in a "gorgeous manner, and they attracted considerable attention." The Louisville Hotel fluttered with flags and blazed with light. The Pearl Saloon, on the corner of Third and Green Streets, had a banner that stretched the length of the building and read "General Rousseau." The National Hotel illuminated with several hundred transparent lanterns, colored red, white and blue. At the end of procession, the citizens of Louisville raised a huge flag over the courthouse, just as they had done in February 1861.[111]

On April 14, Confederate General Joseph Johnston surrendered to Union General William T. Sherman, ending the Civil War. While the city celebrated the great Union victory, a man named John Wilkes Booth strode into President Lincoln's box at Ford's Theater in Washington, D.C., and fired a bullet into Lincoln's brain. After firing the mortal shot, he leaped over the balcony to the stage and rode off into the night. Lincoln died of his wounds on April 15, 1865. Shouts of joy over Lincoln's victory turned to "deep

Brown General Hospital, near Fort McPherson, on the north–south expressway from Eastern Parkway to Barbee. *Courtesy of the National Archives.*

toned words of grief." The nation went into mourning. As Prentice wrote in the *Louisville Journal*: "How terrible the calamity!" Despite Lincoln's errors of administration, he had become the

> *center of public hope and confidence. Though doubtless wrong in some things, he was known to be honest and true of heart... He was the author of new ideas in American politics and the acknowledged leader of a great party, when, as it seemed, there were complications enough to blind the judgment and discourage the heart of any other man...* [Now that the president is dead,] *our reverence for his memory and our sincere appreciation of his many illustrious traits, cause every partisan sentiment we have felt toward him to sink into oblivion. Even as he, while living, was magnanimous and noble toward private and public foes, so we, in view of his calamitous death, would heartily forgive the past, and remember only that which was good and great in the man.*[112]

On April 18, the City of Louisville established a special committee to set aside a day of mourning for Lincoln. The people of Louisville assembled at the courthouse to pay tribute to the memory of Lincoln and renew the expression of their devotion to the government and the Union. Governor Thomas Bramlette presided over the assembly. The large hall of the courthouse was draped in mourning. On April 19, Governor Bramlette, General John Palmer and James Guthrie spoke at the funeral ceremonies. The procession was three miles long. The special committee traveled

A monument to James Guthrie at Cave Hill Cemetery. During the war, he was president of the Louisville and Nashville Railroad.

Another view of James Guthrie's monument at Cave Hill Cemetery.

to Indianapolis to meet the Lincoln funeral train as the train left Washington, D.C., to carry Lincoln's body back to Springfield, Illinois. On April 20, Governor Bramlette ordered every bell in Louisville and throughout the state to toll at twelve o'clock, which was the hour of Lincoln's funeral. All businesses were to be closed and draped in mourning. Every citizen of Kentucky was to pay homage to the national grief.

Chapter 9

The City of Progress

After the nation had grieved for President Lincoln, the military decided to hold a huge celebration for the victorious Union armies in Washington, D.C., in which all the Union Corps marched in a huge parade called the Grand Review. On May 24, 1865, Sherman's two armies, the Army of Tennessee and the Army of Georgia, marched through the streets of Washington, D.C. After the Grand Review in Washington came to an end, thousands of soldiers awaited their return to civilian life. On May 30, Sherman bid his soldiers farewell. The rendezvous point of the mustering out of Sherman's armies would be Louisville. Word reached Louisville that seventy-five thousand Union soldiers would soon arrive in the city. On May 29, the army, under Union General John Logan, prepared to move out to Louisville with seven thousand men at a time. Several members of Logan's staff rode ahead of the army to select campsites in the city and arrange for subsistence.

Union soldiers were not the only soldiers arriving in the city. Many Confederate soldiers arrived in the city, awaiting transportation south. The city rented a building at the corner of Ninth and Broadway to house the destitute soldiers.

On May 10, infamous guerilla William Quantrill stopped at the Wakefield farm in Spencer County, Kentucky, with his men. Captain Edward Terrill's cavalry rode down on his men and a battle broke out. Quantrill received a wound that paralyzed his lower body. Twenty-seven days later, Quantrill died at the Louisville Hospital.

Although many of the infamous guerillas, such as Sue Mundy, One Armed Berry and others, were captured and killed, they continued their robbery, pillaging and murder in Kentucky for many years after the war ended.

In early June, General William Hazen's Fifteenth Corps boarded the first train for Louisville.[113] In June 1865, 96,796 troops and 8,896 animals left Washington, D.C., and headed for the Ohio Valley, where 70,000 men took steamboats to Louisville and the remainder embarked for St. Louis and Cincinnati. The troops boarded ninety-two steamboats at Parkersburg and descended the river in convoys of eight boats, to the sounds of cheering crowds and booming cannon salutes at every port city. Regimental bands blared Civil War tunes. For several weeks, Union soldiers crowded Louisville.

By June 4, the Army of Tennessee had established its headquarters in Louisville. Many soldiers thought the citizens of Louisville received them with a reserved coolness, but they commented that it was a "very nice looking city." One group of soldiers landed between Third and Fourth Street and immediately broke open up a saloon and drank its entire contents. Troops broke into stores and carried away whatever they wanted. Officers had to place guards to stop the looting. The banks of the Ohio north and west of Louisville were covered with tents.

The military organized the veteran regiments of the Twentieth Corps into a provisional division, under the command of General A.S. Williams, and attached it to the Fourteenth Corps, commanded by Union General Jefferson C. Davis. The Ohio regiments, the Fifty-fifth, Sixty-sixth, Seventy-third and Eighty-second, brigaded under General J.S. Robinson and left Washington for Louisville. They arrived in the city on June 20, 1865. According to the Fifth-fifth Ohio Infantry, the division pitched their tents on the Farmington plantation, once owned by John and Lucy Speed and the boyhood home of Joshua and James Speed. The division camped under the great trees at the plantation, which gave the men shade from the hot summer sun.[114]

A favorite campsite for several regiments was the area near the Woodlawn Race Course. On June 27, 1865, Charles Berry Senior, of the Seventh Iowa Infantry, wrote to his father from the Woodlawn Race Course:

Farmington Plantation, located on Bardstown Road, behind present-day Sullivan College. Farmington was the home of Joshua and James Speed. The plantation raised hemp and at one time owned over sixty slaves.

We are still at the same camp ground about six miles east of Louisville. I don't know how long we shall remain here but I hope we shall soon be permitted to go home. Six men of our company are gone home on furlough. The orders are to furlough 12 per cent of the army. I see that some of this army are to be mustered out. I don't venture to say who it may be, nor don't make any calculations, disappointment has already been deep enough but still I hope that we might be once lucky. I hope that I shall get home sometime this summer. It is the general impression that our regiment stands a good chance as they are one of the oldest veteran organizations, only one regiment from Iowa being older, the 2nd I had made calculations of spending the 4th of July somewhere in Iowa but that cannot be. They are making extensive preparations at the Louisville fairgrounds for celebrating the 4th I presume we will be nearer Louisville than Iowa.

While in camp, Berry reflected on his time spent the previous year on the Fourth of July. He wrote that the regiment was on the Chattahoochie, "exposed to shell and bullets while we were throwing up breastworks." He was looking forward to spending this Fourth of July more pleasantly. The weather was warm, and the regiment camped under the shade of beech trees and lounged around in the grass. Berry wrote that the Woodlawn racecourses held trotting matches, and he had the luck of "seeing the fastest horses in America run, one Asteroid that has never been beat."[115]

By June 20, 1865, the city was ringed with thousands of soldiers' tents; the soldiers were restless, tired of war and wanted to go home. Some soldiers felt the wrath of the citizens, who were tired of abuse from Union commanders like Generals Jeremiah Boyle and Stephen Gano Burbridge. The citizens of Louisville had endured four years of soldiers in their city, and some struck out at the soldiers by throwing stones at them or, even worse, shooting, beating or stabbing them. Some of the soldiers were even robbed. The battle-hardened soldiers of Logan's command struck back, and civilians were attacked. The city policemen were shot at as the troops searched the city for excitement. Property damage mounted as soldiers blew off steam and broke into homes or stole streetcars for their entertainment.[116]

Unfortunately, the soldiers took out their frustrations on the local black population. Many black refugees fled into Louisville to escape the poverty of the Deep South and find jobs in the North. The city council asked General Palmer to rid the city of the black refugees, but he refused to comply. Logan's Union soldiers did not feel comfortable with emancipation, nor did most of Louisville's citizens, and many drunken soldiers searched the city for black men to kill. Luckily, there were no reports of Union soldiers killing black refugees, but many suffered beatings. Logan ordered an end to the harassment of blacks.

If the soldiers and civilian battles were not enough, the soldiers began to fight among themselves. Regimental and corps pride reigned over the soldiers, and at the slightest hint that one regiment was better than the other, a brawl erupted in the camps and sometimes flowed into the city. A main ingredient for the soldiers' misbehavior can be traced to one factor: alcohol. Riots in bars and saloons occurred, and many arrests were issued for drunkenness.

Most of the soldiers did not participate in the unruly behavior and maintained their discipline, but Logan decided to issue strict orders limiting the visits to the city, except for urgent reasons. Logan's provost marshals, under Brevet Brigadier General Louis Watkins, numbering five thousand men, patrolled the city. One of the provost guard units, the Seventh Illinois, camped in a vacant lot in the city. To prevent attacks on streetcars, Logan placed guards onboard. One guard stood at the entrance of each saloon.[117] Some of the animosity the soldiers felt toward the local citizens may have stemmed from Kentucky's neutrality and their "sit on the fence" mentality.

Even though seventy thousand Union soldiers caused headaches for the city council and the local citizens, there was a huge silver lining for the city. The United States Paymaster Department paid many of the soldiers their last monthly wages for serving in the army. Some of the soldiers received several months' back pay. With Union soldiers' pockets bulging with Federal money, the city experienced an economic boom. Soldiers visited the Louisville Theater, and the officers stayed in the Louisville Hotel or the National Hotel. They visited the Louisville Casino. Local merchants stocked up on army corps badges, caps and rings. Stores advertised military equipment, such as presentation swords and presentation cased pistols. Local photographers stocked up on photographs of Grant, Sherman, Lincoln and other Union heroes. Local music shops stocked up on printed campaign songs and poems. Merchants sold to government sutlers. Local millineries advertised civilian suits, pants and hats to the soon-to-be soldiers-turned-civilians. Even though the local saloons could not sell liquor to the soldiers, local entrepreneurs went to the camps and sold whiskey.[118]

In June 1865, General Lovell Rousseau decided to run for office for the Fifth District, on the Union ticket. Rousseau won 4,491 votes, Mallory won 1,772 and Mundy won 130.

On July 3, Union General William T. Sherman, known as "Uncle Billy" to the soldiers, visited Louisville. He arrived on a steamer, and a local reception committee met him at the wharf to show him to his lodgings. Soldiers left their camps to see Sherman. The men asked Sherman to speak to the assembled crowd. He responded by saying:

> *Here in Louisville I began the career, which has brought me back here again. Four years ago all was confusion here, and no man knew where his neighbor stood. Four years ago we did not dream of the troubles ahead, but they arose and they are suppressed; and now peace exists all over our land and I welcome back that peace because it appeals to the hearts of men and the highest interests of the nation. I love my soldiers, and I love my fellow officers, but at the same time I think that the interests of the people and country demand that troubles where they arise should be determined by courts of law and not by the sword or musket.*[119]

The next day, Sherman visited the camps and received cheers from his former soldiers. Sherman spoke to the men of their victories, their dead comrades and their hopes for peace and prosperity. Interestingly, Sherman wrote to General Grant of his visit to Louisville and said that he thought many of the men would be bored with civilian life and rejoin the Regular Army.

On July 22, 1865, the Thirty-first Ohio Infantry embarked for Cincinnati, but before they left, they broke into three saloons on the levee and took all the liquor. The next day, the Forty-eighth Ohio Infantry broke out into riot on the wharf.[120] By the end of July, many of the seventy-five thousand Union soldiers mustered out and went home. The military also released all Confederate prisoners of war, with only the guerillas remaining behind bars. Mrs. John W. Green of Louisville wrote in her diary about the release of Confederate soldiers from the prisons:

> *Southern soldiers passed through Louisville on their way home, some of the young girls went to the depot with permission to invite several of the boys home to dinner. Naturally, being immature in judgment, we picked a few whom we thought were nice looking. They proved to be ordinary men, very common and illiterate, much to our disgust. Several of them were overseers, who probably stood*

in with the enemy or, very likely, were Yankees, as the planters often got their overseers from the North. One of our neighbors took a very shabby looking group home with her. She beckoned us to come up to meet them but their ragged appearance did not attract us. We learned afterwards that they were distinguished gentlemen and that "all is not gold that glitters." One of the returning prisoners introduced himself to our father as being his sister's step son, so Father took him home and gave him a position in his business. He was a guest in our house for several years.[121]

By August 1, the Union Army of the Tennessee ceased to exist. By September 24, the military sent all white troops in Kentucky home. During the month of September, the annual State Agricultural Society Fair was held at the fairgrounds on the Shelbyville Pike.

By October 12, President Andrew Johnson's administration abolished martial law.

After the war, four newspapers existed in Louisville: the *Journal*, the *Democrat*, the *Union Press* and the *Anzeiger*. On December 4, Walter Haldeman returned to run the *Louisville Courier*. The *Union Press* was a radical paper devoted to abolition and full rights for blacks. The *Journal* hired C.J. Prentice, George Prentice's son and ex-Confederate colonel, as local editor.

On November 20, the Louisville grand jury indicted General John Palmer for helping slaves escape in violation of the slave code in Kentucky. The reason for Palmer's indictment stemmed from his issuing passes for blacks, who were unable to find employment in the city, to go north. Over a thousand slaves left the city during the first week of June. The city accused Palmer of trying to emancipate the entire slave population of Kentucky. On December 8, the Louisville courts dropped the case, and the next day Palmer revoked all orders relating to passes for blacks.

In December 1865, retired Union General Jeremiah Boyle returned to Louisville and ran the new City Railway. Seventy steamboats were registered in the city. Dr. John Bull's factory on Fifth Street, north of Main Street, produced $50,000 worth of business per month manufacturing sarsaparilla, Cedron bitters, and worm destroyer. Plans were made to rebuild the Galt House on First and Main. The Robert Rowell Electrotype Company was established, which was the first foundry south of the Ohio River. Josiah B. Garthright, a first lieutenant in Confederate General John Hunt Morgan's cavalry, built the saddle firm of Gathright and Company. His cousin, a captain in the Twenty-second Union Kentucky Infantry, joined his firm. Louisville wanted to be the metropolis of the Southwest and tried to attract business.

On December 18, 1865, the Kentucky legislature repealed the Expatriation Act of 1861, allowing all who served in the Confederacy to have their full Kentucky citizenship returned without fear of retribution. The legislature also repealed the law that any person who was a member of the Confederacy was guilty of treason. Additionally, the Kentucky legislature allowed former Confederates to run for office. On December 22, 1865, the city impeached Mayor Tomppert. In protest, Tomppert took the city's official seal so no legitimate business could be transacted in the city. On December 28, the city council chose James Lithgow as the city's new mayor.

On February 28, 1866, Kentucky officially declared the war to be over.[122] Although Kentucky declared the war over, Louisville may not have noticed the change. Louisville became the headquarters for the Military Division of the South, and soldiers remained in the city until the late 1870s. The ever-constant presence of soldiers in the city after the war ended only increased the city's hatred toward military authorities.

What effect did the war have on the city of Louisville? Kentucky historian Thomas Clark commented that the war had two deep and lasting influences. Fathers and sons were divided in their loyalties, brothers fought against brothers and neighbors fought neighbors. Mary Todd Lincoln, wife of President Abraham Lincoln, had a brother, three half brothers and the husbands of three half sisters who fought in the Confederate army, while a brother and a half sister remained loyal to the Union. Unconditional Unionist Reverend Robert Breckinridge had two sons and a son-in-law who fought for the Confederacy. John Jordan Crittenden had one son, George, who fought for the Confederacy and another, Thomas, who fought for the Union. Henry Clay had four grandsons who fought for the Confederacy.

Right: A Confederate monument erected in 1895. The monument has the Confederate seal and is inscribed: "Our Confederate dead 1861–1865." To the left is a bronze figure of a Confederate artilleryman, and to the right is a bronze figure depicting a Confederate cavalryman.

Below: The Frazier International History Museum, located on Main Street, has an amazing collection of side arms and rifled muskets from the Civil War, including editor of the *Louisville Journal* George Prentice's presentation grade Henry rifle and a drum from the Louisville Legion.

Above left: A full frontal view of the Confederate monument.

Above right: The top of the Confederate monument, located near the University of Louisville campus. The bronze figure depicts a Confederate infantryman.

Sixty-seven Union generals from Kentucky fought for the Union and thirty-eight fought for the Confederacy. In all, seventy-six thousand men from Kentucky served in the Union, while twenty-five thousand men from Kentucky fought for the Confederacy. At every Western theater battle, Kentuckians fought Kentuckians. Ten thousand Kentuckians were killed in battle during the war, and twenty-thousand Kentuckians fell victims to disease and exposure. Clark pointed out the startling fact that approximately half the Kentuckians who reached manhood during the 1850s and 1860s were either killed or disabled by the war. The result of the war encouraged "hatreds and enmities ran deep and ruins, spiritual and physical, crippled at least two future generations emotionally."[123]

With so much hate toward the Union military and the Lincoln administration, Louisville citizens embraced ex-Confederate officers, who entered local law, insurance, real estate and political

Above: On the reverse of the monument is inscribed: "Tribute to the rank and file of the armies of the south by the Kentucky Women's Confederate Monument Association, 1895."

Right: A full view of the Confederate monument from the rear.

offices. Ex-Confederates, such as John G. Castlemen, Bennett Young, Basil Duke and J.J. Hilliard, became prominent figures in the business community. Because Louisville dealt with Union soldiers during the entire war and was treated harshly by generals such as Jeremiah Boyle and Stephen Gano Burbridge, Union soldiers did not receive the same acceptance as the Confederate soldiers. As Robert McDowell pointed out his book *City of Conflict*:

> *Louisville was sick of the butchery, sick of the greed of profiteers, sick of rowdy, drunken soldiers, sick of being treated like an occupied city by the Union of which she was supposed to be a part. She had no experience with Confederate armies. The only real combat soldiers she knew were Union soldiers, and these had been inflicted on her for four years.* [124]

Louisville embraced the Lost Cause and saw the Confederate soldiers as fighting a just cause. Louisville searched for regional identity and found the South to be the perfect fit for its needs. George Yater, Louisville historian, agreed with McDowell and stated in his book, *Two Hundred Years at the Falls of the Ohio*, that

> *the impact of the ex-Confederates was out of all proportion to their numbers. Louisville's gradual loss of enthusiasm for the war continued to be a potent factor in the city during the post-war years. In addition, the bitterest memories were kept alive by the continued military presence.* [125]

Louisville erected a Confederate monument in 1895 near the campus of the University of Louisville to honor the Confederate dead. The city hosted two Confederate veteran reunions, one in 1900 and another in 1905.

Appendix

Known Camps and Forts in Louisville

Camp Anderson. Located at the fairgrounds (4th Kentucky Cavalry).

Camp Boone. Located at the fairgrounds and Frankfort Avenue.

Camp Browne. Located near Camp James on Fern Creek (9th Pennsylvania).

Camp Buckner. Located three miles from Louisville at the plantation owned by Simon Bolivar Buckner, commander of the Kentucky State Guard and Confederate General during the War (104th Illinois).

Camp Buell. Located five miles from Louisville on the bluff, also known as Camp Oakland (60th Illinois).

Camp Butler. Located seven miles from Louisville.

Battery Camp. Located between Fort Hill and Fort Saunders, on the corner of present-day Baxter Avenue and Rufer Avenue. Named after Edgar Camp, a captain of the 107th Illinois Infantry who fell at the Battle of Lost Mountain.

Camp Canfield. Located three miles from Louisville (21st Ohio Infantry).

Fort Clark. Located at Eighty-sixth and Magnolia, named after Lieutenant Colonel Merwin Clark, of the 183rd Ohio Infantry, who died at the Battle of Franklin in November 1864.

Camp Dudley. According to the diary of Sergeant Joshiah Feagles, Company G, 3rd Ohio Cavalry, the camp was located four miles from Louisville on the left of the Bardstown Pike.

Camp Eleven Jones Cave. Located on Beargrass Creek.

Fort Elstner. Located near Bellair, Emerald and Vernon Avenues, between Brownsboro Road and Frankfort Avenue, where Beargrass Creek empties into the Ohio River. Named after George R. Elstner, a Lieutenant Colonel of the 50th Ohio Infantry, who died in Georgia in August 1864.

Fort Engle. Located at the corner of Arlington Avenue and Spring Street. Named after Captain Archibald H. Engle of the 13th U.S. Infantry, who died in Georgia in May 1864.

Battery Gallup. Located between Fort Clark and Fort Southworth on part of the old state fairgrounds, named after A.G. Gallup, of the 13th Kentucky Infantry, who died in September 1864 in Georgia.

Camp Hay's Spring. Located near Jefferson County/Bullitt County line on Mt. Washington Road (8th Kentucky and 23rd Kentucky Infantry).

Fort Hill. Located at the St. Louis Cemetery and Goddard Avenue, on what is now Castlewood Avenue. Named after George W. Hill, a captain in the 12th Kentucky Infantry, who died in Atlanta, Georgia, in August 1864.

Fort Horton. Located at the intersection of Shelby and Merriweather Streets, named after M.C. Horton, a captain of the 104th Ohio, who died in Georgia in May 1864.

Camp Irvine. (6th Kentucky.)

Camp Jackson. (13th Ohio.)

Camp James. Located fifteen miles from Fern Creek (9th Pennsylvania).

Camp Jefferson.

Camp Jenkins. Located near Louisville (51st Ohio Infantry).

Camp Joe Holt. Located across the river in Indiana at the Colgate Clock.

Fort Karnasch. Located where Twenty-sixth and Twenty-eighth Streets meet Wilson Avenue, named after Julius E. Karnash, a second lieutenant of the 35th Missouri Infantry, who died in Atlanta, Georgia, in August 1864.

Camp LaGrange.

Camp Laura. Located in the western part of Louisville (113th Ohio Infantry).

Fort McPherson. Located at Preston and Barber Streets, by the old Shepherdsville Turnpike and Louisville Nashville Railroad, south of the old city limits. Named after Major General James McPherson, who was killed in the Battles for Atlanta in July 1864.

Camp Moore. Located near Louisville (25th Michigan Infantry).

Camp Ned Williams. Located five miles from Louisville on the Salt River Road (9th Pennsylvania).

Fort Philpot. Located by the Algonquin Parkway and present-day Seventh Street Road, named after J.D. Philpot, a captain for the 103rd Ohio Infantry, who died in the Battle of Resaca in May 1864.

Fort Saunders. Located at Cave Hill Cemetery, named after E.D. Saunders, of the AAG Volunteers, who died in Georgia in June 1864.

Camp Sherman. Could be the same as Camp Anderson.

Camp Sigel. Located at the south end of Jefferson County (6th Kentucky).

Camp (C.F. Smith).

Fort Southworth. Located in the southwest corner of the city overlooking a sharp bend in Paddy's Run and the Ohio River, named after A.J. Southworth, who died in Atlanta, Georgia, in August 1864. The fort covered nineteen thousand square feet.

Camp (Fort) St. Clair Morton. Located where Sixteenth Street and Hill Street meet, near the point at which Algonquin Parkway and the Seventh Street Road once met. Named after Major James St. Clair Morton, of the Corps of Engineers, who died in the Battle of Petersburg in June 1864.

Notes

Chapter 1

1. Yater, *Two Hundred Years*, 61.
2. Messmer, "Louisville on the Eve of the Civil War," 269.
3. Ibid., 272.
4. McMeekin, *Louisville*, 122.
5. Messmer, "Louisville on the Eve of the Civil War," 250.
6. Ibid., 250.
7. Ibid., 249–50.
8. Ibid., 249.
9. Yater, *Two Hundred Years*, 67–69.

Chapter 2

10. Messmer," Louisville on the Eve of Civil War," 286.
11. *Louisville Daily Democrat*, February 22, 1861.
12. Van Horne, *Army of the Cumberland*, 2–3.

Chapter 3

13. Messmer, "City in Conflict," 84.

14. Military Department of Kentucky, *Military History*, 153; Coulter, *Civil War and Readjustment*, 48.
15. Messmer, "City in Conflict," 84.
16. Edison, "Louisville: During the First Year of the War," 229.
17. Williams, "James and Joshua Speed," 86; Van Horne, *Army of the Cumberland*, 11.
18. Williams, "James and Joshua Speed," 87; Kincaid, *Joshua Fry Speed*, 23.
19. Williams, "James and Joshua Speed," 88; Kincaid, *Joshua Fry Speed*, 24.
20. Williams, "James and Joshua Speed," 89; Coulter, *Civil War and Readjustment*, 89.
21. Clark, *Kentucky*, 128.
22. Messmer, "City in Conflict," 87–88.
23. *Louisville Daily Journal*, September 23, 1861.
24. Eidson, "Louisville: During the First Year of the War," 253.
25. Messmer, "City in Conflict," 117; McDowell, *City of Conflict*, 51.
26. Messmer, "City in Conflict," 117.
27. Messmer, "City in Conflict," 120; McDowell, *City of Conflict*, 51.
28. Messmer, "City in Conflict," 124; McDowell, *City of Conflict*, 53.
29. Messmer, "City in Conflict," 126–27; McDowell, *City of Conflict*, 54.
30. Center For Archival Collections, Rachel Stanton/Searles Papers, Correspondence, October–December 1861, www.bgsu.edu/colleges/library/cac.
31. Messmer, "City in Conflict," 131; McDowell, *City of Conflict*, 55.
32. Center for Archival Collections, Hill/Morgan Family Papers, Guy Morgan to Henry Hill, December 5, 1861, www.bgsu.edu/colleges/libray/cac/transcripts.

Chapter 4

33. Yater, *Two Hundred Years*, 86.
34. Curry, *"Four Years in the Saddle,"* 27.
35. Center for Archival Collections, Hill/Morgan Family Papers, Guy Morgan to Henry W. Hill, www.bgsu,edu/colleges/library/cac.
36. Yater, *Two Hundred Years*, 86; Messmer, "City in Conflict," 131–34.
37. Fryer, *Charles C. McCormick Papers.*
38. Center For Archival Collections, Hill/Morgan Papers, Guy Morgan to Henry W. Hill, Camp Jefferson, Kentucky, January 30, 1862, www.bgsu.edu/colleges/library/cac.
39. McDowell, *City of Conflict*, 60.
40. Ibid., 61; Messmer, "City in Conflict," 134.
41. Eidson, "Louisville: During the First Year of the War," 235.
42. McDowell, *City of Conflict*, 68; Messmer, "City in Conflict," 136.

Chapter 5

43. McDonough, *War In Kentucky*, 114.
44. Fetterman, "1862 Month of Crisis Recreated."
45. Cotterill, "1862—When Kentucky's State Capital was Moved to Louisville," 48.
46. Searcy, "1862 is Remembered as the Year Louisville Panicked Over a "Foreign" Invasion."
47. Messmer, "City in Conflict," 156.
48. Fetterman, "Five Score Years Ago."
49. Ibid.; Messmer, "City in Conflict," 164.
50. Fetterman, "Five Score Years Ago."
51. Ibid.
52. Ibid.; Messmer, "City in Conflict," 169–70.
53. Tuttle, *Diary.*
54. Ibid.
55. Calkins, *History of the One Hundred and Fourth Regiments*, 20.

56. Ibid., 24–25.
57. Ibid., 25.
58. Ibid., 25–26.
59. Ibid., 26–27.
60. Ibid., 27.
61. Boon, *Civil War Letters*, 8.
62. Ibid., 12.
63. Messmer, "City in Conflict," 174; Fetterman, "Five Score Years Ago."
64. "The Murder of General Nelson," *Harper's Weekly*, October 18, 1862.
65. Ibid.
66. Dunlap, *"Your Affectionate Husband,"* 9.
67. *Louisville Times*, September 28, 1962; Fetterman, "Five Score Years Ago, No. 13."
68. Dunlap, *"Your Affectionate Husband,"* 9.
69. Boon, *Civil War Letters*, 13.
70. Ibid., 13.
71. Messmer, "City in Conflict," 174.
72. Fetterman, "Five Score Years Ago, No 14."
73. Messmer, "City in Conflict," 174.
74. Fetterman, "Five Score Years Ago, No. 14."; Messmer, "City in Conflict," 183–84.
75. Fetterman, "Five Score Years Ago, No. 16."
76. "Military," *Louisville Journal*, October 11, 1862.
77. Messmer, "City in Conflict," 199.
78. McDowell, *City of Conflict*, 120.
79. Head, *Atonement of John Brooks*, 155–58.

Chapter 6

80. McDowell, *City of Conflict*, 136.
81. Swiggert, *Rebel Raider*, 116.
82. Messmer, "City in Conflict," 195, 218.
83. Messmer, "City in Conflict," 220; McDowell, *City of Conflict*, 125.

Chapter 7

84. *Official Records*, Series I, Vol. 32, No. 2.

85. McDowell, *City of Conflict*, 159.

86. Yater, *Two Hundred Years*, 92.

87. *Official* Records, Series I, Vol. 39, No. 2, 174.

88. *Louisville Daily Journal*, July 20, 1864, Military Order.

89. Coleman, *Lexington During the Civil War*, 46.

90. Runyon, "Without Cause or Trial," 20.

91. Byron Crawford, "Two Executions in Kentucky aided neither Union nor unity," *Courier-Journal*, May 2, 1980.

92. Runyon, "Without Cause or Trial," 20.

93. McDowell, *City of Conflict*, 166.

94. Byron Crawford, "Two executions in Kentucky aided neither Union nor unity," *Louisville Courier Journal*, May 2, 1980.

95. *Louisville Journal*, July 27, 1864.

96. McDowell, *City of Conflict*, 166–67.

97. Collins, *History of Kentucky*, 137; Head, *Atonement of John Brooks*, 200.

98. *Official Records*, Series I, Vol. 39, No. 2, 244–45.

99. Head, *Atonement of John Brooks*, 200–01.

100. Myers, "Civil War Incidents in and around Meade County"; *Louisville Daily Journal*, "Execution of Guerillas in Meade County," September 6, 1864; Head, *Atonement of John Brooks*, 2.

101. "Execution of Guerillas in Meade County."

102. Ibid.

103. Ibid.

104. Collins and Collins, *History of Kentucky*, 144.

105. Head, *Atonement of John Brooks*, 217–18.

106. Ibid., 203.

107. Collins and Colins, *History of Kentucky*, 146; Head, *Atonement of John Brooks*, 207.

108. Coulter, *Civil War and Readjustment*, 187–88.

Chapter 8

109. Messmer, "City in Conflict," 269.
110. Ibid., 271.
111. *Louisville Journal*, April 15, 1865.
112. Ibid., April 17, 1865.

Chapter 9

113. Jones, "Farewell to Arms."
114. Osborn, *Trials and Triumphs*, 217.
115. Letter from Charles Berry Senior to his Father, June 27, 1865, University of Virginia Library.
116. Jones, "Farewell to Arms," 275; Messmer, "City in Conflict," 285.
117. Jones, "Farewell to Arms," 276.
118. Ibid., 277; *Louisville Democrat*, July 4 and 5, 1865; *Louisville Journal*, July 3 and 4, 1865.
119. Jones, "Farewell to Arms," 279.
120. Messmer, "City in Conflict," 287.
121. McMeekin, *Louisville*, 137.
122. Beach, *Civil War Battles*, 228.
123. Clark, *Kentucky*, 143.
124. McDowell, *City of Conflict*, 204.
125. Yater, *Two Hundred Years*, 95.

Bibliography

Articles

Collins, Richard. "Civil War Annals of Kentucky (1861–1865)." *Filson Club Historical Quarterly* 35 (1961).

Cotterill, R.S. "1862—When the State Capitol was in Louisville." *Kentucky Explorer* 11, 5 (October 1996).

Eidson, William. "Louisville: During the First Year of the War." *Filson Club History Quarterly* 38, 3 (July 1964).

Jones, James. "Farewell to Arms: Union Troops Muster Out at Louisville, June-August 1865." *Filson Club History Quarterly* 36 (1963).

"Louisville Daily Journal Union call to Arms." *Register of the Kentucky Historical Society* 97, 3 (Summer 1999).

"Louisville During the Civil War." *Filson Club History Quarterly* 52, 2 (April 1978).

"Louisville Invaded." *Kentucky Explorer* 10, 4 (September 1995).

Lucas, Scott. "Indignities, Wrongs, and Outrages: Military and Guerillas Incursions on Kentucky's Civil War Home Front." *Filson Club History Quarterly* (October 1999).

Messmer, Charles. "Louisville on the Eve of the Civil War." *Filson Club History Quarterly* 50, 3 (July 1976).

Runyon, Carl. "'Without Cause or Trial': The Story of the Reprisal Execution of Two Confederate Soldiers at Henderson." *Journal for the Liberal Arts and Sciences* 8.

Searcy, Maurice. "1862 is Remembered as the Year Louisville Panicked Over A 'Foreign' Invasion: Second Year of the Civil War Proved to be a Trying Time for All." *Kentucky Explorer* (September 1995).

Speed, James. "Fortified Louisville." *Herald-Post*, March 21, 1936.

Vest, Stephen. "Was She or Wasn't She?" *Kentucky Living*, November 1995.

Books

Beach, Damian. *Civil War Battles, Skirmishes, and Events in Kentucky.* Louisville, KY: Different Drummer Books, 1995.

Boon, John. *The Civil War Letters of John A. Boon of the 85th Illinois Infantry.* 1994.

Brown, Dee Alexander. *Morgan's Raiders.* New York: Konecky & Konecky, 1959.

Calkins, William Wirt. *The History of the One Hundred and Fourth Regiments of Illinois Volunteer Infantry, War of the Rebellion, 1862–1865.* Chicago: Donohue & Henneberry, 1895.

Clark, Thomas. *Kentucky: Land of Contrast,* New York: Harper & Row Publishers, 1968.

Coleman, J. Winston. *Lexington During the Civil War.* Lexington, KY: Commercial Printing Company, 1938.

Collins, Lewis, and Richard Collins. *The History of Kentucky.* 2 Vols. Covington, KY: 1882.

Coulter, E. Merton. *The Civil War and Readjustment in Kentucky.* Chapel Hill: University of North Carolina Press, 1926. Reprint, 1966.

Curry, W.L., comp. *"Four Years in the Saddle": The 1st Ohio Volunteer Cavalry.* Columbus, OH: Champlin Printing Co., 1898.

Drake, Julia, ed. *The Mail Goes Through or The Civil War Letters of George Drake (1846–1918) over eight letters written from August 9, 1862 to May 29, 1865, by the 85th Illinois Volunteer Infantry.* San Angelo, TX: Anchor Publishing Co., n.d.

Dunlap, Leslie, ed. *"Your Affectionate Husband": J.F. Culver Letters Written During the Civil War.* Iowa City: University of Iowa Libraries, 1978.

Evans, Clement, ed. *Confederate Military History*. 12 Vols. Atlanta: 1899.

Head, James. *The Atonement of John Brooks: The Story of the True Johnny "Reb" Who Did Not Come Marching Home*. FL: Heritage Press, 2001.

Johnson, Leland. *The Falls City Engineers: A History of the Louisville District Corps of Engineers United States Army*. War Roundtable Publishers, 1962.

Johnston, J. Stoddard. *Confederate Military History of Kentucky: Kentucky During the Civil War*. E-book on disk, 2006.

Kincaid, Robert. *Joshua Fry Speed: Lincoln's Most Intimate Friend*. Harrogate, TN: Lincoln Memorial University, 1943.

Kirk, Nancy, and Karen Moore. *The Kentucky Book, Louisville*. The Courier-Journal & Louisville Times Company, 1979.

Magruder, Henry, C. *Three Years in the Saddle: The Life and Confession of Henry Magruder: The Original Sue Munday, The Scourge of Kentucky*. Louisville, KY: Published by his Captor, Major Cyrus J. Wilson, 1865.

McAdams, Franics. *History of the 113th Ohio Volunteer Infantry*. Columbus: Chas M. Cott & Co., 1884.

McDonough, James Lee. *War in Kentucky: From Shiloh to Perryville*. Knoxville: The University of Tennessee Press, 1994.

McDowell, Robert. *City of Conflict: Louisville in the Civil War 1861–1865*. Louisville: Louisville Civil

McMeekin, Isabel. *Louisville: The Gateway City*. New York: Julian Messner, Inc., 1946.

Military Department of Kentucky. *The Military History of Kentucky*. The American Guide Series, Works Projects Administration, 1939.

Myers, Dr. Marshal. *Civil War Incidents in and around Meade County, Kentucky, The Terror of the Black Flag: Guerilla Warfare in Meade County.*" Brandenburg, KY: Published by Jane Marlow Willis Wordsmith, 2003.

Osborn, Captain Hartwell. *Trials and Triumphs: The Record of the Fifty-Fifth Ohio Volunteer Infantry*. Chicago: A.C. McClurg & Co., 1904.

Sherman, William. *Memoirs of William T. Sherman*. New York: The Library of America, 1990.

Sifakis, Stewart. *Who Was Who in the Union Army*. Vol. 1. New York: Facts On File, Inc., 1988.

Swiggett, Howard. *The Rebel Raider: The Life of John Hunt Morgan*. New York: The Garden City Publishing Company, Inc., 1937.

Tuttle, John. *The Diary of Captain John Tuttle, Company G, 3rd Kentucky Infantry*. Kentucky Historical Society.

Van Horne, Thomas. *The Army of the Cumberland*. New York: Smithmark Publishers, 1966. Original printing, 1875.

The War of the Rebellion: A Compilation of the Official Records of the Union and Confederate Armies. 128 vols. Washington, D.C.: Government Printing Office, 1880–1901.

Willett, Charles, ed. *A Union Soldier Returns South: The Civil War Letters and Diary of Alfred Willett 113th Ohio Volunteer Infantry*. Johnson City, TN: The Overmoutain Press, n.d.

Yater, George. *Two Hundred Years at the Falls of the Ohio: A History of Louisville and Jefferson County*. Louisville: The Heritage Corporation, 1979.

Dissertations

Messmer, Charles. "City in Conflict: A History of Louisville, Kentucky, 1860–1865." Master's thesis, University of Louisville, 1953.

Williams, Gary Lee. "James and Joshua Speed: Lincoln's Kentucky Friends." PhD diss., Duke University, 1971.

Regimental Histories

Bush, Bryan, ed. *My Dear Mollie: The Letters of Brig. Gen. Daniel Griffin, Commander of the 38th Indiana Volunteer Infantry*. Bedford, IN: JoNa Books, 2003.

Fryer, Larry, ed. *The Charles C. McCormick Papers, Colonel of the 7th Pennsylvania Cavalry, Pennsylvania*. Unpublished, 1997.

About the Author

B ryan Bush is a native of Louisville, Kentucky. He left only to receive a degree in history and psychology at Murray State. He received his master's degree from the University of Louisville in 2005. Bryan has always had a passion for history, especially the Civil War. He has been a member of many different Civil War historical preservation societies, has consulted for movie companies and other authors, coordinated with museums on displays of various articles and artifacts, has written for magazines, such as *Kentucky Civil War Magazine*, *North/South Trader* and *Back Home in Kentucky* and has worked for many different historical sites. He has always fought hard to maintain and preserve Civil War history in the Western theater. In 1999, Bryan published his first work: *The Civil War Battles of the Western Theater*. Since then, Mr. Bush has had published *Terry's Texas Rangers: The 8th Texas Cavalry, My Dearest Mollie: The Civil War Letters of Brig. Gen. Daniel F. Griffin, 38th Indiana Volunteer Infantry, Lloyd Tilghman: Confederate General in the Western Theater, Abraham Lincoln and the Speeds: An Enduring and Devoted Friendship* and *"Butcher Burbridge": Union General Stephen Gano Burbridge and his Reign of Terror in Kentucky*.

Please visit us at
www.historypress.net